PEA SOUP AND JELLIED EELS

Bernadette M Redmond

ISBN-13: 978-1492137276
ISBN-10: 1492137278

Dedicated to Grace Laing who made us go the extra mile

and Eileen Williamson who showed us the way

A memoir of nurse training and life in the late 1950's at St. Andrew's Hospital at Bromley-by-Bow in Poplar, East London, is based on the recollections, training and experiences of the author. In some cases the names of people have been changed to protect their privacy or because they are lost in the mists of time.

Oranges and lemons;

Say the bells of St. Clement's.

You owe me five farthings;

Say the bells of St. Martin's

When will you pay me?

Say the bells of Old Bailey.

When I grow rich,

Say the bells of Shoreditch.

When will that be?

Say the bells of Stepney

I do not know,

Said the great bell of Bow*.

Here comes a candle to light you to bed

and here comes a chopper to chop off your head.

Chip chop, chip chop the last man's dead!

* The 'Great Bell of Bow' in St. Mary-Le-Bow in Cheapside was used to time the executions at the nearby Newgate prison, which for many years were done by means of beheading. The prisoner would await execution on 'Death Row' and was informed by the warder, the night before the execution ' here comes the candle to light you to bed'. The executions commenced when the bells started chiming at nine o'clock in the morning. When the bells stopped chiming then the executions would be finished until the following day!

Table of contents

Chapter 1

Circling the Drain

Following my journey across the Irish Sea on the B&I Ferry, the Hibernia, and a six hour journey on the Holyhead to Euston Mail Train I sat stupefied with tiredness in the tube longing for a peaceful death. I had been met at the barrier by a dumpy, sullen, monosyllabic student nurse, who had been picked on by an all powerful Home Sister to meet the train and deliver me in one piece to her office. Overawed and apprehensive I followed her meekly down into the bowels of the earth taking a seat beside her on the Circle Line Tube. I expected my first Underground journey to Bromley-by-Bow to be brief and uneventful and estimated that a further 15 minutes travel wouldn't kill me.
'Seven stops to Tower Hill' she volunteered. I nodded, too tired to talk. I fell to reading the strip of advertising panels above the heads of the passengers opposite me. Interspersed by maps of the route and 'No Spitting' signs I learned that;

'Rip Van Winkle fell asleep
It was a longish snooze
His clothes indeed were sadly worn but not his Rebuilt Shoes'.

~

'No home remedy or quack doctor ever cured syphilis or gonorrhoea.
Seek free confidential advice at the Middlesex Clinic'.

~

'North, South, East or West, Fry's Cocoa is the best'.

~

'Don't be Fools do Littlewoods Pools'

Eventually my eyes drifted up to the route map opposite just as we came in to Notting Hill Station.
There was definitely something wrong here.

The Circle line was built to join up the main railway termini, had 27 stations on its circular route and was the favourite line, and home-from-home, of the homeless and dispossessed. Most of its route, and all of the stations, are shared by the District, Hammersmith & City, and Metropolitan lines so getting off at Tower Hill and hopping on the District Line to take us further East we should by now have been alighting at Bromley-by-Bow. 'We're going the wrong way round' I told my surly companion whose head was buried in a 'Woman's Own' she had found abandoned on an empty seat. If she had said anything besides 'Oh crumbs' I might have considered forgiving her but my prolonged muttered blasphemous response would have had my Guardian Angel shocked to the core and kept a priest busy for a week deciding on a penance. I later learned it was her day off and that she had not been a willing volunteer.

I had chosen to train at St. Andrews Hospital E3 as a result of a recruitment drive by English hospital Matrons who were in Dublin seeking girls willing to train as State Registered Nurses. I knew that if I applied to any Irish Hospital to do my General Training I would have to pay £200 for the privilege. In the United Kingdom I would be trained free *and* get a salary. Coming to the end of a year's pre training course at St. Anne's Skin and Cancer Hospital I was persuaded by a fellow nurse, Rita Carroll to accompany her to various Dublin hotel lounges to let the Matrons give us the once over. Armed with our training Schedules we presented ourselves for interrogation and scrutiny while consuming the coffee and biscuits provided at each venue. All four Matrons we saw offered us a place 'subject to completion of our course and acceptance by their hospital's Board of Governors', the latter I knew was a mere formality if Matron had given us the nod. It was gratifying and a huge relief to realise our General training was assured. Our futures could be in

Birmingham, Liverpool, London or Manchester. Both Rita and I had been very taken by Grace Laing, the Matron from St. Andrew's in London's East End. Sitting with her and three other possible recruits in Wynn's Hotel I felt she was the only one who had shown a genuine interest in our individual backgrounds and reasons for emigrating. It was also reassuring to be told that she had several ex Probationers from St.Anne's in training and that half of her trained staff were Irish, so Carroll and I both registered an interest in joining the 1957 January set.

What we didn't know at the time was that a goodly proportion of the Ward Sisters appointed before her tenure were less than happy with her views on improving the Hospital regime and nurse training, and of foraging for potential recruits in Ireland and the Dominions. Nearer home her tendency to choose candidates with character and potential meant giving opportunities to girls who had had to leave school without formal qualifications due to the drudgery of family duties. She had to get the Board of Governors on side to do so but since her choices proved their worth she usually got her way.

What I *did* know was that I was part of a generation whose future would be on a foreign shore. Ireland, an impoverished country with a dismal economic environment and De Valera's deeply conservative theocratic government would not be able to meet either our aspirations or expectations in the furtherance of a career. Our exodus was rationalized by many families as a temporary expedient until things improved at home but I was realistic enough to know that my exile would be a long one.

When I informed Sister Mary Joseph, Reverent Mother and Matron at St. Anne's, that I had chosen St. Andrews as a training hospital she vented her displeasure in no uncertain terms. Words like Heathen country, Protestant Hospital, East End slums, Jack the Ripper, Mafia gangs, Marauding Lascars, Opium Dens, Jewish sweatshops and Killer Smog's were all factors mentioned in my misguided choice of training venue. The only things she left out were Oliver Twist's 'Old Nichol' slum (disguised by Arthur Morrison as 'The Jago'), and White Slavers (unless that was what Marauding Lascars got up to?) which led me to believe that her source of reference was more likely to be the News of the World than Charles Dickens or Morrison. She was convinced I would come to a bad end, be 'led astray', might even stop going to Mass or worse still, might marry some heathen in a registry office and be damned for ever; that would be nearly as bad as staying at home and marrying a protestant.

I fulfilled her worst nightmares.

Chapter 2

'Amlets of the Tar'

Tower Hamlets known in the Doomsday Book as 'The Manor of Stepney' had been made up of fishing and farming communities in the hamlets outside the gates of the City of London. This manor was held by the Bishop of London in compensation for his duties in maintaining and garrisoning the Tower of London. The hamlets had now become the Metropolitan Boroughs of Bethnal Green, Poplar and Stepney. They were covered by the mantel of Tower Hamlets again in 1965 when the three boroughs became the London Borough of Tower Hamlets. Nowadays the 'East End' would be deemed to cover the Boroughs of Hackney and Newham as well, and if TV commentators and tabloids are to be believed, extends as far as the nether reaches of the District and Central Lines, particularly if they have something derogatory to report!

The population of the East End has seen constant change from the time of the Industrial Revolution when landless peasants flocked to its Wharfs and manufacturing industries. They were followed by the French Huguenots escaping religious persecution and the Irish famine survivors seeking succour. Towards the end of the 19th century, a new wave of radicalism came to the East End, fuelled by the arrival of Jewish émigrés fleeing from Eastern European vilification, and Russian, Polish and German radicals avoiding arrest. All of those migrants had been accompanied by their families but the newer in-comers were mostly single men who had come in as seamen. These Chinese, Indian, Somali and Bengali Lascars were often paid off and abandoned when ships from the Far East docked. This led to the philanthropic opening of seamen's refuges including the Strangers' Home for Asiatic, African and South Sea Islanders on the West India Dock Road.

Saved from destitution, the Chinese, in particular, brought their families over and formed a substantial community around Limehouse. Canton, Mandarin, Ming, Nanking, Pekin, Streets and Amoy Place are a reminder of Poplar's old "Chinese" quarter.

To designate the three Metropolitan Boroughs loosely as the 'East End' did them a dis-service because they had distinct identities, Poplar (E3), my destination, had its feet in the Thames from the East India Docks at the Lea Estuary to its border up river with Stepney's Wharf's. Stepney, in turn, had the stretch of river up to St Katherine's Docks in the shadow of the Tower.

Post-war Poplar was a very different place to what it had been before the first bombs fell in 1940. St. Leonards Street would never again be the village street with shops serving the Hospital and immediate area. The docks of course felt the worst of the Blitz and the 47 ft long pilotless supersonic V2's when the latter were developed. Regardless of being fully operational and unionised, few dockers had the security of the Button so most still worked on the tally if they were lucky enough to get one on the early morning muster. Women with little or no education, who had kept manufacturing and transport going during the war, were no longer needed and finding getting well paid employment daunting, many opted for a teen-age marriage and motherhood. Vermin infested slums still housed hundreds of young couples and overcrowding was a way of life; and while family life was close, families were large. Girls, a few miles down the road in Newham fared better finding work in Silvertown's Tate and Lyles sugar refineries and Keiller's jam and marmalade factory along the Docks.

Bethnal Green Borough (E2), with its big weavers windows shared a border with Hackney and was an altogether more indigenous settled area, with little more than street names and surnames hinting at the antecedence of its Huguenot, Irish, and

English silk and linen weavers. With Stepney, it also shared a boundary with the City of London so had a history of trades practiced outside the City Walls. This included a red-light district of Jack the Ripper fame trailing down Quaker St. and Brick Lane as far as Spitalfields, then controlled by Maltese pimps and eventually the local Krays.

The Borough of Stepney (E1), renowned for its tailoring and schmutter, was recognisable by its Synagogues and multinational Ashkenazi Jewish population who mostly undertook their own welfare services. Ashkenazi refers to Jews of East European origin but the earliest Jewish settlers in the UK were Sephardi who arrived in the C17th at the time of Cromwell and were refugees from the inquisition of The Roman Catholic Church. Jewish tanning and clothing industries covered the main Whitechapel commercial thoroughfare and surrounding streets as far as the City Wall at Aldgate where the miasma of noxious industries such as abattoirs, tanning and lead smelting had historically been located beyond the walls of the City. Apart from its warehouses and access to the East India Dock and Limehouse Basin the Isle of Dogs which made up most of E14 was a marshy backwater built on the Thames flood plain so likely to flood in any abnormal tidal surge. With its poor transport connections nobody bothered about it, little realising its prime situation until the expansion of the brokerages in the City began looking for sites for development turning it into a 21st.century power zone.

So along the Tower Hamlets length of the tideway of the wharf's, docks, basins, piers and quays of the Thames you could be in Hong Kong, the slums of Kiev, the ghettoes of Warsaw, or seeking the short lived 'delights' of the ladies of the night around Christchurch in Spitalfields. With a Seaman's Mission in your neighbourhood you had the added cultural experience of its inhabitants gathering together transporting you to Somalia,

Bengal, India or other outposts of the British Empire where Lascar labour was cheap. Inhabitants of the Salvation Army and other Hostels for the Homeless were more familiar being ex-services Tommy's or Irish or Scots navvy's who had lost their way in life. All being down and out their major difference was not their ethnic origins but the fact that the former did not have drink issues.

The immediate problem for the East End after WW2 was to house families whose homes had been bombed. War damage had been repaired by 1953 and attention shifted to slum clearance. The Greater London Council invested in building purpose built blocks of flats but by 1957, with the coffers of the Treasury empty, skeletons of houses, demolished streets and warehouses waiting for repair and renovation were still the playground of local children. There were also surprising patches of green turned into allotments by nearby residents. At night the light from Gotchies coke fires glowed in the dark hiding the signs of neglect and deprivation as they sat in their night watchman's hut guarding sites from pilfering or arson.

Housing was allotted to those in cleared areas rather than by a waiting list. About 5,000 people lived in temporary housing, including requisitioned properties and 'prefabs'. Some of these much loved chalet type prefabs with their own little gardens were still in service half a century later.

Kinship, never seen as a key dimension of people's lives by planners moved the rest out to new overspill towns such as Beaconsfield and Debden in Essex. The inhabitants considered electricity, inside loos and bathrooms and their own front doors poor recompense for the lack of camaraderie amongst neighbours and the loss of community they had to endure. A far reaching plan for redevelopment, involving the demolition of whole streets and roads continued, and the building of high rise flats, underpasses and overpasses have since changed Poplar radically and all that is left of St. Andrews is memories.

Chapter 3

The 'Orspital

'Why are you boring us with all these historical references' you ask? Well, dear Reader, in case you hadn't noticed this is a memoir not a novel so if you are expecting Mills and Boon cease reading now. Moreover it is a memoir of training at a time and place in a much loved institution that after several reincarnations has been razed to the ground. While this is only a 'snapshot in time' my grandchildren have criminally negligent teachers who have not encouraged them to choose history as a GCSE subject so have as much knowledge about life in my youth as would fill a 2"x4" screen on an iPod. As my Gran was wont to say 'You don't know where you're going unless you know where you've been' so just a few more historical facts before training gets underway.

St. Andrew's Hospital in Devon's Road was founded in 1868 next to the site of the old Stepney Workhouse. Under the Metropolitan Poor Act of 1867 it was renamed the Poplar and Stepney Sick Asylum when it opened in 1871. The Asylum was renamed St Andrew's Hospital in 1921 when it became the responsibility of the London County Council. It remained an Asylum until 1933 before becoming part of the National Health Service in 1948. The 1941 bombing of the Poplar Hospital for Accidents which stood on the East India Dock Road at the entrance to the East India Docks saw St. Andrews emerge as a District General Hospital for Poplar. With 750 beds the General Nursing Council accredited it as a training school for State Registered Nurses and Part 1 Midwifery.

The formation of the National Health Service resulted in the closure of many of the East Ends small specialist hospitals which had been endowed by well known philanthropists or subscribed to by the local population who could ill afford the small fees. The

NHS was free so the philanthropists either closed their premises or handed them over for use by the NHS. Well into the 1950's General hospitals waited until a new field of work was well established before providing specialist beds. So while Consultants shared Wards, opening and staffing new Departments took longer and were usually the prerogative of the Teaching Hospitals with Medical Schools attached. The subdivision of medicine into specialties, taken for granted today, was then still in its infancy. Concentration on fields narrower than general medicine or general surgery met with resistance within the NHS which was striving to get rid of specialist hospitals and specialist nurse training. At that time there were about 25 state recognised courses whose nurses staffed the specialist hospitals, the most established of which were sanatoriums, lying-in hospitals, hospitals for fevers, orthopaedics, children and ophthalmology. A few provided services to particular groups of patients - Italians, French, Germans, and Italians and Dockers. Some were religious foundations, others only dealt with particular illnesses or organs, like the Lock Hospital, in Soho, in the West End with facilities for the treatment of venereal diseases.

Besides St. Andrews in Poplar the only other hospital of any comparable size in the East End was The London Hospital in Stepney. Fronting the Whitechapel Road it gloried in being the recognised Teaching Hospital for the area. It was not long before I realised we were in direct competition with their well spoken middle class girls from the shires who regarded nurse training as a finishing school, the prize being finding a young Doctor to marry.

Back on the tube the Underground District Line became a surface service from Bow Road so as we pulled into the Bromley-by-Bow stop abutting the station was the grim Victorian pile that was St. Andrews Hospital. Bounded at the front by Devon's Road with St. Leonards Street to the rear, and surrounded by its original asylum type wall, this redbrick Victorian building with its imposing three, four and five storey gothic facades looked very daunting when exiting from the tube entrance in Devon's Road for the first time. Built along architectural lines that favoured the lock down asylum type pavilion system of separate blocks, each block was connected by side verandas, corridors and bridges. This system also reduced risks of cross contamination on wards that accepted isolation cases for assessment.

A central administrative block contained Matrons Office, the muraled Board Room, the Lady Almoner's domain, Administrative Offices and a Chapel, with the kitchens and laundry rooms at the rear. Along the main corridor were the three-storey ward blocks of 28 bedded Florence Nightingale wards. Looking down the length of the long corridor their ground floor recessed entrances were hidden from view with a lift and stairs serving each block. The impressive wards were 13' wide by 12' high making them light and airy and with enough draft potential to kill all but the most resistant germ.

Although the Hospital could be accessed from St. Leonards Street the back entrance was used primarily for deliveries and as an emergency exit and fire evacuation station. Entering from Devon's Road entrance ones eye was immediately drawn down the length of the long shiny parquet floored vaulted corridor that faded into the distance, ending at the double doors of the Maternity Block that straddled the end of the corridor. Many a pregnant woman in the throes of labour would curse the architectural decision to put the Labour Ward, at this end of the hospital and many a breathless porter cursed it too as he charged along pushing a wheelchair with a bellowing woman.

'Make way Nurse, m-a-k-e-w-a-y, m-a-k-e-w-a-a-a-y'

'Ead in knickers 'ere' was the cry, shouted with an urgency that couldn't be denied.

St. Andrews Wards were not named after beneficent benefactors or Worshipful Companies. They were simply named alphabetically, identified by an unadorned letter of the alphabet and an arrow indicating direction. With about 24 Wards some letters of the alphabet were not used but at this passage of time I can't remember which they were. Despite the starkness of alphabetical designation we found a means of identifying them in our own irreverent way according to speciality;
Maternity was 'Obs and Gobs',
Gynaecology was 'Saints and Sinners',
Surgery was divided into three specialities; Gastro intestinal was 'Guts and Butts', Gallbladders and breasts 'Chole's and Tits' and Thoracic was 'Drains and Chains'. The latter was a bit obscure but denoted being confined to bed attached to drainage tubes. Chest drains also known as under water sealed drains (UWSD) were inserted to allow draining of the pleural spaces of air, blood or fluid, allowing expansion of the lungs and restoration of negative pressure in the thoracic cavity.
The Renal and Genito-Urinary ward was 'Rene Riddle'.
Geriatrics* was Chroni Bronies,
Paediatrics was 'Happy Campers', if the children were in the croup tents; 'Spots and Dots' if they were in the infectious section, or 'Fits and Nits' if they were in the main Ward.
The TB and other exotic diseases Ward was 'The Penal Colony'
General Medicine rejoiced in the name of 'Monolulu Land'.
The Orthopaedic Ward had the most derogatory name of all and was named after a local Hardware shop, 'Sankey's'; the specialists in this field being regarded as overpaid carpenters. For Wards that had male and female allocation the name was followed by the word male or female so 'Sankey's' was 'Sankey's Male' or 'Sankey's Female'.

Disliked sisters were derisively called Fanny instead of Sister. However we did have 'The Duchess' who, with an Office wall full of newspaper clippings, lived off her moment of fame when she was introduced to the Royal Family during the Blitz. We also had 'Queenie' on Rene Riddle named after the Queen in Alice in Wonderland whose staff nurses spent their time covering their backs because of her skill in never accepting blame for anything. There was also Blondie and Dagwood a husband and wife team, and Big Bertha, built like a Scythian warrior and named after a 12 calibre type Howitzer gun.

This purulent humour was our way of coping with daily exposure to injury, disease, emergency situations and death. Also we were among Cockneys renowned for their rhyming slang and well known dialect that only used 24 letters of the alphabet, 'h' being silent and 't' replaced by a glottal stop e.g. 'ot wa(t)er. I will refrain from trying too much to represent dialect and spoken accent in print except when it is simpler to do so.

Our Consultants were also christened with highly unsuitable nicknames; Mack-the-Knife (enthuastic experimental surgeon known for his Whipple's procedure and suspected of been willing to experiment on his own granny),

The Butcher (an enthuastic but incompetent surgeon whose wife would not allow him carve the Sunday roast).

The Rear Admiral (gastro-intestinal specialist), and The Plumber (urologist) both of whom turned the toughest dockers into quivering wrecks.

God's Gift (gynaecologist) whose bedside manner and limpet brown eyes had even the elderly prolapses swooning, but then, they never witnessed his spectacular temper tantrums in theatre.

The Witch Doctors or Juju men (medical consultants) dabbled in the dark arts and were revered by all.

We also had Woolworth's (Casualty),

The Carvery (operating theatres), and
The Carpentry and the Humpty Dumpty Departments (orthopaedics and physiotherapy) who put people back together again.
I mustn't forget the Tod Sloan Suite also known as St. Peters Waiting Room (morgue and viewing room), and next door The Padre (the pathologist who performed the 'Last Rites').
Our Paediatrician we called the 'Randy Dandy' which had nothing whatsoever to do with his specialisation having more to do with his Saville Row suit, flamboyant bow ties and his propensity to brush against student nurses breasts or stand too close behind them. *Far too close.*

Our Porters and Maintenance staff also had memorable monikers such as;
'The Don' Head Porter and procurer of hard to get equipment (no names, no pack drill),
Cherub (butter wouldn't melt and Dons front man),
Big Frank (he who must be obeyed … trained apprentices)
Daisy (renowned for his highly polished army boots)
Red Jack (Union Rep whose favourite word was demarcation)
Sunshine ('now give me a nail and a hammer'… jack of all trades and Red Jack's nightmare)
Micky Bliss (annoying joker and piss taker)
Elvis (spotty look-alike and later Flu Epidemic Saviour)
Twinks (not so secret ballroom dancer and smart dresser)
Ger (who did beautiful embroidery and lived with his Mammy)
Lofty (wheelchair champion renowned for his Labour Room dashes)
And on nights;
Dodger (never to be found)
Noddy (always finding a quiet corner to doze)

Gene Kelly (whose Vold hobnail boots woke half the hospital as he clipped clopped along the corridors like a Shire horse).

Staff Nurses without a designated ward and student nurses filling gaps in training requirements were called Floaters or Slaves. Aptly named, because the former were treated like flotsam and jetsam until a permanent post came up. Although the bondage of slavery had been abolished in 1833 the latter were slaves to the whims of the Sister of whatever ward they were on as their duty rota changed from day to day and they couldn't call their lives their own.

*Geriatrics was not then a speciality.

Chapter 4

Nurses Home

Parallel to the railway track was a large Nurses Home its extensions from a smaller Victorian building evident. It was affectionately known as 'The Nunnery' less affectionately as 'Ollaway' after Holloway a well known women's prison. Both fallacies were perpetuated by the belief that we were locked in at night when in fact we were locked out! Originally Victorian it had been added to pre and post WW1 to accommodate the needs of a general hospital. The Minton floored entrance hall gave way to dark parquet and an overall impression of being gloomy, musty and highly polished. To the right was a frosted glass door with the stark word Office etched at eye level. The surly one knocked and I was introduced to Home Sister, and her Deputy, who doubled as Infirmary Sister.

Dressed in long sleeved navy blue uniforms with narrow white lace collars held in place by ornate Hospital Badges and the ensemble completed by frilly caps they looked like disagreeable twins; and from their frosty faces, clipped English accents, to their black lace up court shoes they could well have been. I was handed over to their care and spent the next half hour being given the tour by the Deputy as well as a lengthy familiarity with the 'Rules and Regulations'. Not an iota of consideration was given to my welfare after such a long journey. Not one single enquiry of a personal nature was asked. My need to pee was becoming desperate, and once relieved, a cup of tea wouldn't have gone amiss afterwards.

Eventually I was taken to my bedroom on the second floor. I cheered up immediately. How wonderful it was to have a room of my own. There was a single bed facing the window, a fitted unit with desktop and wardrobe along one wall, a lovely warm radiator under the window, a bedside cabinet and light, a straight-backed chair and delight-delight a full length mirror. Eat your heart out Sr. Agnes! The latter, a Nurses Home Sister at St. Anne's, had regarded vanity as one of the seven deadly sins ensuring that there hadn't been a single full length looking glass in the Home. However she was a kindly guardian of whom we were all very fond. I don't think I was ever going to say that of Tweedledum and Tweedledee.

Notwithstanding the advent of rock and roll, life in the 1950s was a time of conformity and marked by conservative values. The age of majority was 21y but nurses started training at 18y so Matron and Home Sister had an almost quasi-legal guardian role over you while you were training. They had control over when, and how, you wore your uniform, your appearance, when you were allowed out and how late you could stay out, and had no qualms about contacting your parents if your moral welfare was at risk.

To ensure that temptation and the occasion of sin were minimised a ten o'clock curfew was imposed on first years. What would be new to me was the hierarchical nature of the nursing staff at St. Andrews.

I learned that in the dining rooms, staff sat at tables allocated by their rank. So, as a first-year junior nurse, you sat with other first-year low life before progressing to the second tier of tables the following year and so on until you became a Staff Nurse. Sisters had their own dining room. This pecking order continued on the Wards but there was more opportunity for student nurses to mingle in the Nurses Home Sitting Rooms. This was where nationality took precedence over rank. Guilds of religious groups were also fairly free from hierarchical separation although newbies were supposed to behave like mushrooms i.e. be kept in the dark and have sh*t piled on any views expressed. A year hence I was to start down the road to perdition at a League of Catholic Nurses meeting.

Once you had passed your State 'Prelims' at 15 mths curfew was extended to 10.30 and you were allowed, with your parents permission, to move out of the Home and live in digs. Nurses who 'lived out' still used the building. They all had lockers in a room in the basement. When they went on duty they kept their gabardine coats and bags in their lockers where they also stored their clean uniform. We had to wear clean aprons every day so dirty laundry was put into laundry bags, also kept in the locker and sent off to the laundry on our designated weekly laundry day, issued by the position of your surname in the alphabet. When we worked on night duty, which was quite often then, we had to congregate in the Sitting Room for Night Sister to take a Roll Call and confirm our Ward allocation. In the main corridor down near the locker room there were information boards. Their official purpose was to display Exam results, Holiday lists, Church services, and free Theatre tickets, however over night these would be buried under flyers for Dance Halls, Invitations to Police, Fire Brigade, or Medical Students Socials, or exhortations to join the local Communist Party all removed as soon as Home Sister's eyes were cast upon them. One of her missions in life was to catch the perpetrators.

Chapter 5

The School of Nursing

Part of my tour around the residence included instructions to make my way to the Dining Room at 12.30 for Lunch when I would be given information about how my afternoon would be spent. While these instructions had reached my ears they had not penetrated my cerebrum so I was just psyching myself up to go back and ask the dastardly duo to repeat the directions when there was a smart rap on my door and I opened it to find my fellow Probationer from St. Anne's, Rita Carroll, knuckles raised to knock again. All 5'1" of her with curly black hair, neat little nose and pale freckled Celtic skin, she stood there grinning from ear to ear her Co. Monahan accent a joy to hear.

We compared journeys and our induction.

'Jezzis, what did ye think of Bette and Joan' she asked making herself comfortable on my bed.

'Aren't they a scream'?

She had no idea how accurate her description was. I had appraised them as a united force whose intent would be to make our life in the Nurses Home a misery, but I learned, in time, that despite a superficial front they were in deadly competition with each other, and delighted in scoring points denigrating each other's performance. They were also not fans of Grace Laing's modernising outlook.

'Don't they just remind you of C. J.? I asked, remembering our Nemesis at St Anne's, a bully of a Nun whose cold gray eyes had bored holes in us in an effort to humiliate and intimidate us into submission. Known as Creeping Jesus because of her silent approach she constantly caught us at our worst which made me a firm believer in the component of Murphy's Law that says

'Success occurs when no one is looking, failure occurs when Sister is watching'.

I also firmly believed that I was cursed.

We spent the next few minutes catching up before making our way to the Dining Room talking nineteen to the dozen. We were met at the door by a red haired sister dressed in like fashion to the Home Sisters but with a red grosgrain belt clasped by an ornate silver buckle. A clipboard in hand she merely raised her eyebrows enquiringly. Guessing what was required I responded 'Redmond and Carroll, Sister'. Finding our names she directed us to one of two tables of girls in mufti like us.

'Be sheated andwait tobe sherved' she told us in a fast Cork accent. Rita and I tried not to smile. Nearly the whole of the Nursing Staff at St. Anne's had been from Cork and both of us, me from Dublin and her from Monahan, had struggled for months to understand the dialect. The Cork and Kerry habit of interchanging 'y' and 'r' was confusing. While they use the plural 'ye' like most culchie's in the singular it becomes 'rou' instead of 'you'. They also interjected 'h's' everywhere but particularly after the 's' and 'st' sounds so that sleep became shleep, and stop became sthop. But worst of all was the way they ran words together without taking a breath. I won't go on writing in this vernacular because it will drive us all mad; just take my word for it that you get used to it.

After lunch were all taken over to the Preliminary Training School. More familiarly known as The PTS or the 'Potting Shed' we would be nurtured and pruned here for the next six weeks before we undertook examinations to assess whether we had the makings of a nurse and more importantly that we were safe to be let loose on live patients.

There were seventeen of us in the January set. Number eighteen balked at the last minute and efforts were being made to replace her since we would be spending a lot of time working in pairs. Having all being introduced we discovered we were from Ceylon, India, Ireland, Jamaica and N. Ireland or more succinctly 9 Prods, 8 RC's. The staff of the PTS comprised of Miss De Souza, Curriculum Tutor and Mr. George who specialised in Fevers and Psychiatric conditions. There was also a rolling programme of student tutors who gained teaching experience on us. Eileen Williamson the red haired Cork Sister we had already met was a Clinical Practice Teacher. Not that we would have dared call her Eileen to her face. She was always Sr. Williamson or more affectionately 'The Road Runner' because of her quick smart military pace. Eileen's role, newly created but not yet established, had been funded due to Grace Laing's foresight in providing teaching on the Wards as well as the blocks of learning in the School of Nursing. Eileen therefore walked a tightrope between the all powerful Ward Sisters and our Tutors in the School of Nursing.

Miss De Souza was a plump little Anglo-Goan-Indian with bottle-top glasses, droopy jowls and the hint of a moustache and Mr George who was ex-army Medical Corps Tutor had the most massive teeth I have ever seen outside of a museum with displays of Neanderthal cave men. These magnificent gnashers caused him to shower those nearest to him with droplets of spit, and worse, if he didn't rinse his mouth after lunch. While neither they nor the Ward Sisters could best Eileen when it came to clinical practice and knowledge, she had no Tutoring Diploma which put her on a pay scale below the Tutors but on par with Ward Sisters. However Eileen was a born teacher and it would be her who moulded us into the nurses we would become. We were to learn that a look of disapproval from her was far worse than a tongue lashing from a furious Ward Sister.

The Potting Shed was an annex with a ground floor space the size of an empty ward and adjoining offices that had served as military accommodation during WW2. There was talk that it had been the ECT and seltzer bath room in its Asylum days. It was separate from the Hospital in that it was self contained so we saw nothing of hospital life apart from the dining room and the Nurses Home. However we appeared to be downwind of the hospital kitchen who's industrial size catering seemed to be forever belching out enticing smells of food which never lived up to expectations. One half of the PTS was set up with tables and chairs for lectures and small group work, the other half like a ward with several beds and space for learning practical skills. There were two glassed cubicles set up for learning the requirements of barrier nursing and sanitation of a Milk Kitchen and the four small side rooms used as offices by the Staff. The walls of the main room displayed great illustrated anatomical schemata of the ten major organ systems including one depicting the male reproductive organs which had the riveted attention of seventeen sets of virginal eyes upon it. Well, I'm assuming we were still innocent of close scrutiny of the real thing.

Having shown us around Sr. Williamson opened a cupboard door and wheeled out a skeleton with a screw embedded in his skull to keep him upright and display his 206 bones. Amidst nervous squeals and giggles she gave us a killer look and informed us that the gentleman in question had donated his body to Science and that we were to handle him with the utmost respect and if she found anybody desecrating him (Jezzis, what did *that* mean?) she would personally see to it that our days at St. Andrew's, would be, de facto, numbered. I saw several of the RC's blessing themselves and wondered if anybody had ever prayed for his soul. I remembered the Widow-Maker Hickey at St. Anne's, my first and only 'sudden' death which had happened in the last week of my training. To everything there is a season, even a time to die from a terminal illness, when patients would receive 'The Last Rites', so for any patient inconsiderate enough to die before their allotted span we were issued with a card with a' Prayer for the Dying' typed on it. I had carried around this card in the back of my note pad for a whole year for just such an occasion, and apart from using it once, prematurely, much to the consternation of Paddy Joe Delaney having an afternoon nap, I did my duty by Seamus Hickey's immortal soul as he sat on a toilet seat, pyjama bottoms around his ankles, and his perpetual cigarette (despite being in the last stages of Mesothelioma) still dropping ash down the front of his vest.

Introduction to the PTS completed we were taken over to the sewing room for uniform fitting. We had sent measurements by post so there should be little to do but adjust the length. However having been issued with mid calf length dresses when I started at St. Anne's I wasn't too hopeful that I wasn't going to end up looking like a Victorian skivvy again. The previous problem had been quickly solved by my mentor Theresa Donovan and a packet of custard creams for Maggie the sewing room arbiter of Sr. Agatha's 'two inches below the knee' length. Custard creams made a couple of inches disappear leaving Sr. Agatha with no evidence of illegal tampering. I was therefore mightily pleased to find the dress lengths absolutely spot on but poor Rita was swamped in yards of blue and white striped cotton. Somebody had misread her 5'1" for 5'11'! Back to the Dining Room for tea we were allowed to disperse to our rooms for the evening to sew Cash's name tapes on our stack of uniform which comprised

7 dresses

10 aprons

7 collars

4 caps

1 red lined black cloak
1 Navy Gabardine belted coat
1 Navy Gabardine hat
The list of personal possessions I had been expected to bring

1 pair of Clarks black lace up shoes / or
Similar from any well known nursing range
3 pairs of black serviceable stockings
1 fob watch with second hand
1 pair of regulation nurse's scissors
2 drawstring laundry bags
3 dozen Cash's name tapes

had been modest in comparison to the one I had had to acquire before being accepted at St. Anne's which resembled nothing so much as a trousseau, leading Annie Lawlor, our next door neighbour to exclaim

'Holy Mudder a' God', 'you'd think youze were entering a bloody noviciate'.

So clothes and books unpacked and suitcase stowed away on top of my wardrobe I was too tired to feel homesick and was asleep as soon as my head hit the pillow.

Chapter 6

Matron

Although I was aware that the railway track ran parallel to the Nurses Home I had not expected to find that my bed rocked in time to the rumble of the passing tubes or that I would awake in the wee small hours to the constant clink-clank clink-clank of long wagons of cars leaving Dagenham's Ford Assembly Plant en route to far off distribution points.

Heading to the Dining Room I was not in the best of moods and having already endured an overcooked lunch and dinner I was not expecting a cordon bleu breakfast. Industrial size kitchens working to a budget produce inedible splodges that can sometimes be identified by smell or colour; sometimes it can't, so you eat it anyway. Hungry, but not desperate I joined sixteen uniform clad newbies.

'Porridge or boiled egg' one of the Dining Room maids asked.

I can't recall my choice because in reaching for some bread I noticed there was no butter on the table just a plastic container of luminous yellow margarine.

'There's no butter at breakfast' somebody told me.

Eight pairs of consternation filled Irish eyes looked at the informant, a compatriot, not believing their ears, or the evidence of their eyes.

'You have two pats at teatime otherwise its marge' she further informed us.

'My sister and cousin are here and they made me bring them butter from home' she sighed as only a downtrodden younger member of a Clann knows how.

I had only ever been offered marge once before in my life, that was when Beatrice Murphy invited me to tea as a child. Even then I hadn't got any further than smelling it before feeling queasy.

There was no way I was ever going to get used to it. I would rather starve.

Over in the Potting Shed we were scrutinised from head to shoe by 'The Road Runner'. She looked grimly at Rita Carroll, Mary, the youngest of the O'Brien sisters and me. Our white starched caps, which were meant to cover as much of our hair as possible, were crimped and folded to about half the designated size and perched rakishly on the crowns of our heads. However she couldn't fault our hair tidily off our faces and collars which was no small accomplishment with Carroll's bouncing curls. The other 14 looked like orphans in a storm. She was a woman who fought her battles wisely. She could have made the three of us conform, thereby losing the war, because within a week we would be emulating our predecessors artistic creations anyway, instead she handed us a card of white hair grips and set us to making the others fit for presentation to Grace Laing who was about to descend on us. She continued with her inspection examining us for evidence of make-up, scent, jewellery, and nail varnish. Some fell by the wayside failing the shoe polishing standard and length of finger nails but by mid morning when Grace Laing arrived we would have passed muster with the pickiest of Sergeant Majors.

I had never seen Grace in her Matron's regalia. In Dublin she had been one of the twinset and pearls brigade. At 53y she was a good looking fit woman. Her Celtic skin, name and hint of an Edinburgh accent denoted Scottish ancestry though she had been reared in Battersea South London. Dressed in navy blue serge her white collar and elaborate lace cap was her badge of office. Her enamel hospital badge adorning her dress showed she had trained at the 'Hammersmith'.

I waited in some trepidation for her welcome speech having vivid memories of the one I got when I started at St. Anne's. However Grace's was a far cry from Sr. Mary Joseph's who having invited me to be seated while she had sat behind her imposing desk, had talked at length about the vocational nature of nursing, the need for personal discipline, long hours, seemly behaviour, purity of heart and mind, and our duty to provide spiritual as well corporal care to our patients. My acceptance by St. Anne's was an honour I was told, and I should offer up my duties to God, his Crucified Son and Blessed Mother by performing them to the best of my ability. I also got a lecture on 'Aspirations' which I thought was about what my plans were only to discover she was talking about developing the worthy habit of offering one line prayers to God, Mary and the Heavenly Hosts of Saints as I went about my duties.

Grace's welcome by comparison was secular in tone. This was somewhat surprising because a lot of hospitals at the time, including The London in Whitechapel, started the day with Ward Prayers. She told us that;

"By undertaking to train at St. Andrews a door of opportunity had been opened waiting for you to start a journey which will lead to endless opportunities. Your State Registration will be recognised worldwide and will also be a foundation stone for further specialisation. My hope for you is that you will have the wisdom to demand the best from yourself because we, most certainly, will stretch you to the limits of your endurance because our standards of patient care are exacting. The path you are choosing demands character forming perseverance and diligence. Success does not belong to your parents your mentors or your tutors, it belongs to you. We will help you along the way but the rest is down to you. I have been a nurse long enough to realise I am not talking to a band of angels and that each and every one of you will be sent to see me at some time, however what you also need to know is that my Office door is open between 8.00 and 9.00am weekday mornings to anybody who wishes to see me."

I knew that notwithstanding the fact that there was no butter at breakfast I had made the right decision.

Chapter 7

Communal Health and Dietetics

As nursing students in the 1950s, we were taught every aspect of hygiene from hand washing through barrier nursing to scrubbing up. Our chapped hands bore evidence of the vitriolic cleaning materials in vogue at the time. Having already had a good grounding in Bacteriology at St.Anne's it came as no surprise to me to discover, that like God, germs are everywhere. As unauthorised stowaways they are in your body, in the air and in your food and drink. You can't breathe, eat, have a cut or use your hands without transporting them. The least said about the exchange of germs during kissing the better.

Sr. Williamson and Mr. George were very innovative when it came insuring the Set's introduction to Microbiology and Public Health. With that in mind we went trooping out to the Express Dairy major creamery and milk bottling plant located just south of Acton. This location gave easy and equal access for milk trains from both the Great Western and the Southern Railway lines. Our hosts took us through the process of pasteurization with great enthusiasm proclaiming the wonders of High-temperature-short-time (HTST) pasteurized milk which we were told had a refrigerated shelf life of two to three weeks, whereas ultra-pasteurized milk can last much longer, sometimes two to three months. When ultra-heat treatment (UHT) is combined with sterile handling and aseptic packaging it can even be stored unrefrigerated for 6 to 9 months. He had obviously never lived in a Nurses Home otherwise he could never have been able to test this theory because theft from the landing communal kitchens was rife! For those of us who liked milk in our tea our standby was a pierced can of evaporated or condensed milk in a jam jar on the window sill. The jam jar was to prevent the inventive sparrows from getting at the small wodge of paper used to seal the opened tin.

In the HTST process, we watched the milk being forced between pipes heated on the outside by hot water, and reaching a temperature of 161°F for 15–20 seconds before being bottled. In the UHT process the milk was held at a temperature of 275° for a minimum of one second. Like later Domestos ads these processes were designed to kill 99.9% of all known germs, dead! This is considered adequate for destroying almost all yeasts, moulds, and common spoilage bacteria and also to ensure adequate destruction of common pathogenic, heat-resistant organisms such as *Mycobacterium tuberculosis*, the cause of tuberculosis, but not *Coxiella burnetii,* which causes Q fever, a serious relapsing disease which, I learned, the United States investigated as a potential biological warfare agent in the 1950's!

Our Communal Health excursions took us to unexplored parts of London not normally on the tourist trail. The first stop was Hackney and a visit to the sewers. Descending the ladder to the platform overlooking the Northern Outfall Sewer's epic tunnel at the Water Boards Wick Lane Depot we waited for the aroma to hit. But much to our surprise there was only a hint of turd. The rest was a mixture of North London ripe detritus coming into the Outfall from sewers converging at this meeting point, and thence to the pumping station at Abbey Mills and on to the treatment works at Beckton.

Abbey Mills, a Water Boards pumping station near Stratford was an enormous intricately ornate rococo building designed to resemble a mediaeval fortress with keep and bailey and battlements and large stepped buttresses all around. Its interior was spectacular and with an organ and pews could have doubled as a cathedral. All of inner London's sewers north of the Thames met at Abbey Mills from where waste was pumped to a sufficient

height to allow gravity to draw it away to Beckton. When the Metropolitan Board of Works pioneered London's sewage system in the years from 1848, Beckton was considered far enough down river to be designated as the drainage outfall for sewers north of the Thames, with equivalent works at Crossness serving the area south of the river. Here, until 1887 waste was released untreated into the Thames at high tide or stored in a reservoir at low tide.
The building of the sewage treatment works at Beckton comprised a liming station, precipitation, settlement and storage tanks and a jetty in the Thames from which the solids were transported to be dumped out at sea; the cleansed liquid was discharged into the Thames. Following our visit to Abbey Mills we went on to Becton to see the engine room, boilers and architecturally prized chimneys which powered the machinery involved in moving the sludge through the treatment process. Although several miles apart the pumping station and sewerage works were joined by the Greenway embankment (the original main drain) that ran between them.

Having enjoyed a nice afternoon out without bothering to take note of the intricacies of the processes we were being shown you can imagine my horror when the main question on our Communal Health and Hygiene exam asked me to explain the processes that occurred between flushing a lavatory to turning on a tap. Glancing around the classroom I could see I was not the only one looking like a startled rabbit.
Likewise our session at the milk plant was not without repercussions as we had to list the procedures involved in looking after a Milk Kitchen on a Paediatric or Post Natal Ward. I waffled my way through infection control, aseptic techniques, sterilizing, measuring, labelling, and temperature control. Discussing the exam results later Eileen Williamson's caustic remarks were not lost on me and were reflected in the mark I got.

'A mention of the germs you are intending to decimate in this elaborate plan wouldn't have gone amiss' she noted wryly. If the truth be known Rita and I was cruising through PTS having already done a year's nursing, and she knew it.

Also part of our PTS curriculum was our two mornings a week at the Poplar Tech learning 'Elementary Chemistry' and 'Dietetic Values and Invalid Cooking'. The former dealt mostly with the chemical components of urine testing and mysteries of Tincture of Guaiacum, Ozonic Ether, Benedict's Solution and Acetic Acid. We also learned about renal and liver function tests.

The Nutrition lessons resurrected memories of my 'Domestic Science' class at school and brought a lump to my throat recalling bringing home my cooking efforts for the Gran to praise and poor long suffering Granda to eat. The woman taking the class in the Tech advocating that 'Food should be chosen, cooked, garnished and served to tempt the appetite' had obviously never eaten at St. Andrews. My memories of her cookery course are vague and involve setting pretty trays, adjusting portion sizes and choosing the colour of plates, however I did find her advice on serving invalid food with a view to encouraging appetite useful when I was allocated to the Penal Colony.

Chapter 8

Surgical Nursing

Our last week in the Potting shed and the notice board showed everybody had passed the PTS Exams. Next to it was the list telling us which wards we were being allocated to. Nancy Kavanagh, a neat little girl from Kilkenny and I were down for 'K' Ward; at the time, a male surgical ward treating mostly gastro-intestinal problems, so also known as Guts and Butts. This mostly entailed patients being subjected to laparotomy incisions from sternum to pubes to 'take a look'. This surgical incision through the abdominal wall was made to allow investigation, and hopefully, diagnosis of an abdominal disorder, or at its worst, cancer. No thought was given to the resultant aesthetics of such a massive scar. The other common procedure was a proctoscopy which involved a large instrument up the anal canal, and although it left no physical scars our male patients, given a choice, would have opted for the laparotomy!

After the 16 bedded wards at St. Anne's the wards at St. Andrews seemed so big with their high ceilings, long windows, and dark wooden parquet floors. Inside a Ward door was Sisters glassed in Office, and half way down each ward was a long solid wooden table for serving meals to ambulant patients. A break in the bed spaces contained a wash hand basin, and with clearance all around it, a substantial wooden medicine cabinet with an eye level top for measuring potions. Apart from that the 28 beds and lockers were equally spaced with all the shining bed casters turned inwards. Two rows of beds with mitred corners, nice taut blue counterpanes hanging equidistance, with a 16" fold of sheet measured from fingertip to elbow were every ward sister's unachievable dream. Bed occupants circumvented this dream on a daily basis unless they were on their way to St. Peters Waiting

Room, but even then, their grieving relatives often unthinkingly sat on the bed creasing the pristine counterpane.

The sluice room and ward facilities with their white tiled walls were discretely out of sight at the end of each ward. Too discreetly, as it proved when a suicidal patient took a flying leap out of a third floor bathroom window during my second period of night duty. He was lucid enough to close the bathroom window behind him leaving his discovery to a young member of staff coming on duty early the following morning.

Although Sr. Hall (aka Blondie) was a mean spirited little woman the standards of patient care on her Ward were exacting and no task was too menial. Nearly all Ward Sisters were unmarried but unusually Blondie broke the mould and was actually married to the Charge Nurse on Ward B, known as Dagwood, Blondie and Dagwood being a well known comic strip at the time.

I already had a year's expertise in bed making, bedpan rounds , pressure area care, taking blood pressure and temperature readings counting pulse and respiration rates, intake and output measuring, serving meals, arranging flowers, packing autoclaves and sluice cleaning so could have been an asset to the Ward, but I was left in no doubt that, while I had already gained proficiencies in these tasks I would now do them under the supervision of a third year until I was considered a safe practitioner. Aseptic techniques, bed bathing, giving enema's and injections, testing urine and participating in medicine rounds were also now way outside Sisters hierarchical expectations of my lowly status. However I *was* allowed to be a dirty nurse. An unfortunate name I know but a 'dirty nurse' helped to change dressings. I boiled all equipment, cleaned the trolley with methylated spirit, placed a sealed autoclaved pack on top and a covered bowl underneath and wheeled it to the bedside. I then pulled the curtains, exposed the dressing and washed my hands. The sterile nurse (an equally unfortunate name), having explained to the patient what happening waited for me to open a pack of sterile gloves which she donned while I opened the sterile dressing pack. I removed the soiled dressing with a forceps and discard it into the bowl underneath the trolley. This procedure was repeated until all dressings were completed. It was desperately galling to stand by having been deemed capable of changing dressings at St. Anne's especially as it had been Sr. Josephine who had signed my proficiency having instilled in me a fanaticism about preventing wound infection.

Limehouse Lil, so called to differentiate her from Jamaica Lil on H Ward, who had never been further than Jamaica Street in Stepney, was our Ward Maid and was worth her scrawny weight in gold. Five foot nothing and without a pick of meat on her she regularly sucked her yellowing teeth in exasperation when I got under her feet. She was the proverbial fairy Godmother who stretched the tea ration to the limit of drinkability, served meals, replenished water jugs, washed up, kept the kitchen and bathrooms clean, damp dusted the bed frames, lockers and windowsills daily and also polished the long table. She Ronuked the floor once a month then buffed it once a week to a shine using a cumbersome 'dummy'. This was long handled block of wood the head of which was covered in pieces of old blanket to apply the polish and then another piece of blanket to make the floor shine. The force of the 'thump thump' of the dummy was a good indicator of Lil's mood. Polishing was usually done after bed making on the first Saturday of the month and created a major upheaval. We all helped out pulling beds into the middle of the room for the sweating red faced Lil and woe betide a patient who asked for a bedpan or bottle at this time. When I say we all helped out it goes without saying that Sr. Hall always had that week-end off!

Lil had a contentious relationship with Blondie. As far as Lil was concerned 'K' Ward' was *her* Ward and believed Blondie was merely an administrator who could be replaced overnight, while the Ward would fall apart without *her*. There was an element of truth in this since we never missed Sister on her day off but we certainly missed Lil. Patients were noticeably crankier as the relief Ward Maid never remembered their little preferences, or forgot to replenish their water jugs, and we had to have eyes like hawks making sure she didn't tempt the 'nil by mouth' pre-op patients because Lil never had to be told.

As I became familiar with Ward routine I learned that no one entered a ward without a Ward Sister's permission apart from Matron and the particular God who had beds there. Patients rested after lunch so visiting rules was strictly enforced and visitors stood in a line in the corridor until Sisters hand bell was rung at 2.00pm and in they filed two to a bed. No children were allowed without special permission although if the patient was well enough to go out on the veranda visiting out there was not policed. However, Nancy, a surreptitious smoker was always keen to wheel patients out there, or check on their needs, evidence of her solicitousness being noticeable on her mint flavoured breath. On the dot of 4.00pm the bell was rung again and the visitors decamped. The next lot went through the progress again between 7.00pm and 8.00pm with no lingering good-byes tolerated.

It didn't take me long to butt heads with Sr. Hall.

Chapter 9

The Egg and Spoon race

I was to learn throughout my training the Ward Sisters came in all shapes and sizes, colours and creeds, and abilities and idiosyncrasies that ranged through the good, the bad and the mad. Sr. Hall was a dolly mixture. She ran a good ward regime but meanness was a vice that percolated through her pores leading to badness and the madness of the unhinged. Since this was my first ward it took me several weeks to realise we were not like other wards, and it was Limehouse Lil who brought it to my attention and precipitated the Oliver Twist incident. Breakfast, served by Lil and the student nurses was a choice of porridge or boiled eggs with patient's choice varying very little from day to day so a dozen or so would choose boiled eggs. The problem with this was that we only had six teaspoons so patients further down the ward had to wait for the first six to eat their eggs and for us to collect them and re-wash them. This sounded so petty that I couldn't believe it, but it was the thin end of the wedge.

The ward kitchen was a fully equipped good size room. It was Lil's domain and as clean as an operating theatre. She took charge of the sliced loaves, milk, margarine and eggs delivered daily from the main kitchen. Lunch and Dinner were delivered by hot trolley also from the main kitchen and served onto plates by Sister or Staff Nurse. No matter how much food was left over it was more than our careers were worth to eat even a mouthful. It led to instant dismissal. The weekly delivery of loo rolls, soap, tea, coffee (for Consultants only), cocoa, horlicks, jam, biscuits, soup and other sundries to tempt a sick appetite were signed for by sister and put under lock and key in her Office. On any other Ward Lil would have been trusted with a duplicate key to the

Office storeroom to take a daily ration of tea etc but Blondie trusted nobody so created endless aggravation by insisting on doling it out herself.

'*Why have we only got six teaspoons'* I asked Lil after a particularly fractious breakfast when a patient trying to suck out the contents of a soft boiled egg had got most of it down his pyjama top while I arm wrestled another for possession of an eggy spoon?

'Because that mad bitch is convinced that they will be stolen' she answered nodding at Blondie. Hmm.

Now we're not talking family heirlooms here or solid silver service, not even stainless steel. We are talking cheap nickel plated spoons engraved with NHS on the handle which would proclaim to all and sundry that the possessor of an ill gotten spoon was not only a thief but a pretty moronic indiscriminate one at that. And why concentrate on tea spoons when there was a full complement of equally grotty knives, forks, and dessert and soup spoons?

'She has a drawer full of them in her Office' Lil told me sensing an ally.

For all of thirty seconds I considered the rashness of what I was about to do before knocking on Blondie's door. Opening the door before being invited to do so I had the advantage of finding her sitting at her desk dunking a biscuit in a cup of coffee.

Her face froze with annoyance but before I lost my nerve I went into my Oliver Twist mode and informed her that six teas spoon on a ward of 28 patients meant a great deal of inconvenience to everybody concerned so could we please have some more. Unlike Oliver and the Beadle I could match Blondie pound for pound even as she inflated with rage before my eyes. I had so far survived better huffers and puffers than her (ah, fond memories!) so I stood my ground as she blow dried my hair, but could not get her to even consider my request.

Lil, with her ear to the door scuttled back to the kitchen in fright.

'Gawd, Reds, you are a one and no mistake' she whispered in a tones of awe mixed with terror.
'The bitch will make your life a misery while you're on the Ward'.
Was there a hint of vicarious relief in her sympathetic performance? Well, whatever the motive I knew that what she said was true. Was I going to cave in and accept defeat achieving nothing but Blondie's torture? Was I hell!
Throwing caution to the wind and ignoring an inner voice urging a cooling off period I took Grace Laing at her word that she was available to all between 8.00 and 9.00am and made for her office during coffee break. The door, identified with the word Matron was ajar. My limbs turned to lead as I raised an arm to knock.

A simple 'Come in' found Grace Laing behind her desk looking at me expectantly. No hiding behind paperwork or other power tactics I had her immediate attention and enough scrutiny to make me wish I had put on a clean apron. I'd like to think I was succinct, articulate and to the point but I know that I was wishing I was anywhere but this gracious panelled room so I'm sure there was some amount of stammering and stuttering.

'Do you wish Sister to know you have brought this to my attention' was the only question I remember her asking during her inquisition?
'Yes' I replied, remembering the slaying of previous dragons. But I discovered Grace Laing had her own way of doing things.

An early morning Matron's Ward round was unheard of but there she was on 'K' Ward at 7.30am the following morning just as we were about to serve breakfast. Blondie, in her Office was totally oblivious to the fact until Staff Nurse gave her the nod. Her agitation was sublime as she tried to divert Grace into her Office away from the breakfast trolley but Grace's determination to follow the trolley and talk to the patients won the day. She observed the egg and spoon fiasco at first hand and following the trolley back to the kitchen examined our bare cupboards as an ecstatic obsequious Lil bobbed and weaved around her. I knew Grace, having decided to deal with the situation this way would make no mention of my complaint, but I also knew from Blondie's narrowed eyes and clamped lips that she had worked it out. The outcome was that she had to disgorge 22 teaspoons from her hoard and increase the amount of tea and sugar for the odd cup of comfort for a poorly patient.

I was punished by being given four split shifts a week instead of the more usual two. I made no complaint but Eileen Williamson took note because of the amount of times I had had to cancel clinical supervision. I expected a dire report when my allocation was up but it was non committal and brief just in case anybody would look for bias.

It would not be my only run in with Sr. Hall.

Chapter 10

Medical Nursing

While Orthopaedic Surgeons were held in some derision as overpriced carpenters or mechanics there was a great deal of respect for the General Medical Consultants or 'Witch Doctors'. Monolulu Land, as the medical wards were known, was named after a local character Ras Prince Monolulu. One of the best-known and flamboyant London showmen who pitched up at Stepney's Petticoat Lane market every Sunday was a black racing-tipster who grandly called himself Ras Prince Monolulu. He claimed to be a chief of the Falashati tribe of Abyssinia but the reality is that he came from the Danish Caribbean island of St Croix His catch phrase "I Gotta Horse, I Gotta Horse" was as famous in its day as any current one you can name. He was usually decked out in an ostentatious head-dress of beads and ostrich feathers, a techni-coloured dream waist coat and harem style gaiters. He also wore a selection of silk scarves wrapped around his waist and was hardly ever without his huge shooting stick-cum-umbrella.

In an era when x-rays and fluoroscopes were the only means of seeing inside a patient. barium swallows to show up a heart, in black and white contrast, were common. The Jujumen's skill lay in history taking and physical observations that involved smelling and tasting (!), palpation and osculation, reading ECG's and quantifying blood gases with a Van Slyke's machine. Chest Physicians dealt mainly with the treatment of rheumatic heart disease, syphilitic heart damage, and infective endocarditis. Treatment of resultant heart failure consisted of good nursing care and bed rest because digitalis and mercury-based diuretics such as mersalyl given by injection were the only medications available. Until the discovery that year of chlorothiazide, the first effective oral diuretic, regular hospital admission was inevitable but now meant they could theoretically live a much more normal life, at home, while under treatment by the GP and District Nurse. Ten years too late for my 39y old mother who, following four pregnancies in quick succession had died from heart failure as a result of rheumatic fever and resultant mitral stenosis.

Treatment for hypertension and coronary heart disease was also in its infancy so nursing and rehabilitating 'stroke patients', some in early middle age, was also part of daily ward life. Hospitalization, bed rest, and the prescription of Antacids and 'bland' diets for the treatment of peptic ulcers was another bed blocker. Gastro-intestinal Physicians focused their attention primarily on diagnosis by barium meals, tarry stools and taking early morning gastric fluid samples from patients with suspected ulcers. The latter was achieved by passing a nasogastric tube up a fasting patient's nose down into the stomach making them retch as it passed into the oesophagus. This was a job for medical students who had to get out of bed at the crack of dawn to get the sample. As student nurses we were all capable of carrying out the procedure and sometimes took pity on a particularly dishy student if he failed to get there before the early morning tea round because we knew the patient would drink the tea and ruin the fasting sample. Medically, antacid therapy was the treatment of choice for peptic ulcer disease while the Surgeons wanted to slash out the offending organ.

Leila Lackey, a lanky anorexic looking Belfast Prod, with a voracious appetite was allocated to Monolulu Land (Male) with me for an enjoyable three months and we became great friends.

Under the leadership of one of Grace Laing's appointed Sisters, Sr. Brooke, the ward was well run with a fair distribution of split shifts and week-ends off. Initially I missed the excitement of surgical nursing but soon found that medical nursing could be immensely satisfying. Special diets and Intake and Output charts were as important as post-op drains and infection control, however while patients co-operated with surgical care they regarded nutritional prohibitions as fair game for circumventing. Diabetics were probably the most difficult to treat but the worst offenders were patients with oedema from heart failure, or ascites from failing livers or kidneys. But all patients on restrictions were treated as recalcitrant, devious conniving little sods who would sell their mothers for a bowl of Jellied Ells, a jug of Whelks or a plate of Pie and Mash. It didn't help that Tubby Isaac's had a stall by the 'Bird in Hand' on route to the Hospital. I also suspected that Cherub (butter wouldn't melt) had a hand in supplying late night treats from the stall. Nowadays when I watch 'reality' TV shows on morbidly obese people who can't even wipe their own bottoms my first question is not *who* is feeding them but *why*? In our instance the *why* was too far into the realms of psychodrama to ponder, so our way of dealing with patients who were showing no signs of improvement was to enforce 'Operation Seek and Destroy'. This process went from giving visitors information about their loved ones condition and the reasons for restrictions, to 'Stop and Search' at the ward door if we suspected contraband.

Patients, failing to improve, had bedside lockers raided to scowls and growls of 'Ye'r worse than a bleedin' Screw' or we had to listen to them casting aspersions on our legitimacy or chastity.

If we were searching for drugs, alcohol or tobacco I could understand their ire but making a fuss about a helping of Jellied Ells or Pie and Mash was beyond my comprehension. If we could control their intake of protein, salt and potassium and periodically tap their ascites we could successfully control their symptoms in the hope that future intervention might be possible, which was very rewarding from a nursing point of view, but obviously did not warrant giving up the Foods of the Gods on their part. If I had a penny for every time I was told 'Jellied Ells don't do no one no 'arm' I could have had enough to splash out on an Aer Lingus flight home at the end of my three month allocation.

While the aforementioned premise is debatable the *smell* of rotting fish leaves no room for disputing its potential harm if only to our gag reflexes.

On an Indian summer day in September the Ward windows were open wide to allow the warm air to circulate and to try to waft away the putrid smell of rotting fish. Three days of vigorous cleaning had failed to locate it tho' it had been whittled down to one particular corner. Every department with the remotest possibility of tracing its origin came to examine, smell, swab, disinfect, spray and pontificate.

It was Big Frank (He who must be obeyed) who solved the mystery. Unlike the others he did nothing on arrival except sit on a chair facing the corner. Like a radar operator he scrutinised every inch of the area in his range of vision without moving, his two trainee acolytes at attention behind him. Life on the Ward came to a grinding halt as none of us wanted to distract him. Even the Head Juju man and his entourage paused and then stood still as we all waited with bated breath. After what seemed like an eternity Frank stood up, went over to the bed in the corner and switched on the anglepoise lamp. Nothing happened. His two apprentices moved to his side, the junior one carrying the bag of tools. Like any great surgical God he held out his hand and the senior apprentice selected a screw driver from the tool kit and reverently handed it to him. He carefully unscrewed the large round wallplate for the lamp. As it came away the stench of liberated rotting fish in an unmistakable Tubby Isaac's single portion container was revealed. The gut wrenching odour rolled out like a miasma hitting the gag reflexes of all within a ten foot radius.

It was obvious our Search and Destroy Mission had missed that one! We were fairly certain we knew who the culprit was, and more importantly, we would be seeing him again. As my Gran's neighbour Annie Lawler would say

'Never mind the mills of the Gods, just give me the little bowzie for a few minutes and you can have his guts for garters'.

Chapter 11

TB Nursing

On return from a month's holiday in Ireland which was spent sleeping, eating and trying to circumvent inquisitions about boyfriends I found myself allocated to B Ward the male Tuberculosis Ward aka The Penal Colony. So named because, under the Public Health (Control of Disease) Act patients suffering from communicable diseases could be forced to take their medication by supervised administration or involuntary inpatient treatment. Tuberculosis has plagued humanity for a long, long time. The ancient Egyptian King Tutankhamen died of it as did a long list of other well-known characters; Fredrick Chopin, Stephen Foster, John Keats, Robert Louis Stephenson, the whole of the Bronte family and many more. In many parts of the world TB or the 'White Plague' still reigned as one of the most opportunistic of all diseases. The introduction of Mass X-ray vans and routine Heaf testing children at the age of 13y showed the extent to which asymptomatic infection was occurring in the community. The effectiveness of treatment, particularly in early cases, was an added reason for identifying patients as rapidly as possible.

In the late 1950s, the standard treatment for pulmonary TB was the administration of isoniazid and para-amino salicylic acid (PAS) for between 18 months and two years, along with newly discovered streptomycin for the first three months. Statistical comparisons between sanatoria and home treatment showed that treatment in sanatoria of sputum free from infection patients was no better than at home, and thus contributed to the closure of the TB sanatoria by the end of the 1960s. However non compliance became a problem until effective short term medication became available so relapsers ended up in our Penal Colony to ensure compliance under supervision. Little thought was given at the time by the medical staff for the reasons for non-compliance. Charge Nurse Hall, (Dagwood) a time server and man of limited capabilities, assumed it was simply a matter of patients choosing not to follow advice, failing to recognize, that choice may have been severely constrained by their social circumstances.

Public Health contact tracing through active follow up of those exposed to TB and other communicable diseases, was critical in preventing re-infection and ongoing transmission of susceptible individuals. The service was the responsibility of the District Medical Officer and was well established in East London and much more in tune with patient's home circumstances than the hospital staff were. TB thrived in poverty, insanitary conditions and overcrowded housing and among hostel dwellers, the homeless and vagrants. I found days on the Ward were both boring and cold. There was a full length open air veranda were bed bound multinational patients were nursed, and a section with easy chairs for ambulant and moderate rest patients to sit and congregate. I seemed to spend most of my time encouraging patients to eat, playing cribbage measuring sputum, filling hot water bottles as the weather got colder and taking my cardigan on and off. We were allowed to wear a uniform cardigan on the Ward but not when engaged in nursing care, so figure it out. As Micky Bliss, our resident joker was accustomed to say

'Cor blimey Nurse, that cardigan is on and off more times than a tom's drawers'.

The rest of my time was filled enforcing 'No Smoking' rules on infinitely stubborn patients who had failed to quit.

There was a weekly ward meeting between the Head Juju man, the Lady Almoner and the Medical Officer to plan discharges, and at which contact tracing and recidivists were discussed. As a consequence of Grace Laing's innovative training the student nurses on the Ward spent a day a week with the Community Nurses working out of Social Services. We all looked forward to this. It was our one opportunity to see inside the patient's homes, hostel room or dormitory thereby putting flesh on the bones of their lives outside the hospital. Brenda Gallagher, the Health Visitor who took me on my weekly day out took everything in her stride including putting her foot through a rotten stair thread in a dark dank multi occupied hovel. I felt her 'Drat, I've ruined my nylons' did not do justice to the situation. However she had a great rapport with the families and patients she visited, advising with common sense, praising when called for and firm about compliance and a down to earth approach to which they responded.

Born and reared in Summerhill in Dublin I was familiar with tenement dwellings but it would have been hard to beat some of the squalor around the backstreets of Stepney, our most disease ridden area. However it was not all doom and gloom because there were pockets of reasonable housing usually on the Peabody and Guinness Estates if artisans could afford the rent, or in harder to get East End Dwelling Company or the Jewish endowed Industrial Dwelling's Company which housed the families of day labourers.

My overall impression of our forays into the community was of trying to avoid yards and stairwells full of washing lines with flapping clothes and the inquisitive youngsters whose curiosity and cheek knew no bounds. We never had to knock on a door having been already heralded by shout up the stairs of *'The Woman from the Welfare is 'ere'.* This proclamation was shouted in various tones of voice from dire warning as when announcing the Rent Collector, exasperation, if the timing of the visit was inconvenient, or in optimism if re-housing was on the cards.

Occasionally Brenda came across instances of domestic violence and neglect but the majority of her caseload was decent families, who like the families around Summerhill, brought up their children in dire poverty. While their children, at times, may have been cold and hungry, and may not have had money for material possessions they provided solid stable homes which few of their children would judge inadequate. These families would always make do, helping out the neighbours when they could, knowing that the kindness would always be repaid.

Notwithstanding the improvements in TB recovery rates the dread of 'consumption' was still rife, so home visiting was discrete, and often cloaked in other welfare issues, examining drains being top of the list. One young Jewish widow, Rebekkah, we were visiting was beyond saving and was literally dying from exhaustion, but was still trying to earn a living as a seamstress while her mother looked after her two young children. Despite her extreme thinness her flushed cheeks gave her a vicarious illusion of health. Because of the nature of her illness she would not let Brenda approach the Jewish Welfare charities on her behalf so the inevitable happened and she died from a massive haemorrhage the day before our next visit. Her death was inevitable but her demise could have been a lot easier for her and her little family if the secrecy and shame surrounding tuberculosis could have been overcame.

Chapter 12

Pea Soup

The winter smog's in London found fame in the books of Victorian and Edwardian authors as well as menacing black and white films of the era. Caused by a meeting of air borne sulphuric oxides from soft inefficient bituminous sea coal mined off the Northeast Coast, and moisture in the air from clean natural fog it became lung corrosive sulphuric acid smog. With the right weather conditions it could last for days and was lethal to vulnerable people such as the elderly, the very young and those with respiratory problems. The pungent smell of acrid sulphur hung about in the atmosphere making your eyes smart and lungs emit explosive fits of coughing.

Smoke from millions of chimneys combined with the mists of the Thames Valley meant that people in low lying East London, with its high polluting factors, feared a Pea Souper as much as their families had Jack the Ripper in the 1880's. Memories of the peace time catastrophe three years before when 12,000 or more Londoners died as a result of four day smog was still fresh in people's memory and the establishment of the Clean Air Act the previous year brought no reassurance. Most locals could not afford the more expensive anthracite coal so continued to use sea coal while stocks lasted.

My first East End experience of smog came in late November. Walking became a matter of shuffling my feet to feel for the kerb and despite making progress with my arms out like a sleep walker to avoid obstructions I managed to walk into a lamp post. Venturing out in the premature gloom was made even worse because each back street lamp at the time was fitted with an incandescent light bulb which gave no penetrating light onto the pavement to see my feet, or even the lamp post! Fog penetrating fluorescent street lamps had not reached Devon's Road. Living alongside the over ground railway line there were frequent bangs near the signal stand beside the track. These explosions were made by percussive caps which were used as fog signals and were placed on the track to warn drivers that they were slowly approaching a signal, and that they were to stop the train and peer out at the signal through the smog to check for clearance to proceed. When the smog eventually cleared away everything was covered in sooty grime. This grime stayed there until it rained. God never did a very good job on the Hospital leeward windows so we lived in gloom until the six monthly cleaning.

The Lewisham train crash on Wednesday 4th December 1957 was entirely due to smog and mitigated by the lack of an Automatic Warning System. The accident occurred during a spell of cold and very foggy conditions that caused severe disruption to train services in the London area. The resultant smog is thought to have been especially dense in the cutting between New Cross and St John's, with the driver of the 5.18pm electric train from Charing-Cross to Hayes reporting that visibility was reduced to 20 yards or less in some places. Due to uncertainty of the signaller in Parks Bridge junction signal box as to the destination of the electric train he held it at a signal soon after St John's station. It stopped with its last carriage under the flyover which carried the Lewisham to Nunhead line. A few minutes later, at 6.20pm, it was hit from behind at about 35 miles per hour by the delayed 4.56pm steam train from Cannon Street to Ramsgate. The ninth and tenth coaches of the ten-coach Hayes train were telescoped together, with the ninth riding up over the under frame of the eighth destroying it completely. The tender and first coach of the steam train were derailed and struck one of the supports of the Lewisham-Nunhead flyover. The flyover buckled immediately and collapsed onto the first three coaches, crushing two of them almost flat. Further disaster was narrowly averted when the driver of a train about to cross the flyover noticed that it had buckled and managed to stop short. The first coach of this train was tilted over at an angle, but did not fall onto the wreckage below and was evacuated quickly and hauled to safety. Ninety people were killed and 173 injured and in an era before Mobile Disaster Teams, Helicopter Rescues and Health and Safety Assessments, the Fire and Ambulance Services, with the aid of the Police Force to guide them through the smog, had all survivors extracted and in hospital before midnight. As a matter of interest it took another four decades and several more train disasters before an AWS was made mandatory on British Rail, whereas the benefits of the Clean Air Act which had became Law the previous year would abolish smog within a decade.

Although Lewisham was across the River in South London hospitals on both sides of the Thames felt the repercussions of the disaster as the great bed swap began. St. Andrews within sight of the entrance to the Blackwall Tunnel in East London, and a further ten minutes or so to the crash site on the other side was designated to free up beds in Lewisham Hospital to allow them to treat the casualties. Because of the Tunnel under the Thames we were also less affected by the smog, allowing the transfers fairly rapid access. The only problem was we had very few empty beds and even fewer patients fit for discharge as the freezing smog had ensured our Chroni Bronies had filled every bed in the chronic Wards. Grace Laing instigated a full Fire Drill as the only means of alerting us all to the coming mayhem and those of us off duty went back to our rooms to get ready to go back on the wards. We were under no illusion about the calibre of patients we would be receiving from Lewisham. They would take the opportunity to get rid of 'bed blockers' and so it proved.

However we had Grace Laing and 'The Don' in the splendour of full uniform, masterminding the reception at our end.
Not an ambulance went out through our gates with a scrap of equipment still on board. As far as Grace and The Don were concerned if a patient was delivered with an oxygen tank, drip stand, arm splint, wheelchair, blanket and pillows they ceased to be Lewisham General Hospital or Ambulance equipment but were sequestered as the patients possessions necessary for their welfare, any disputes to be settled at a later date. Two years later the porters were still pushing wheelchairs around with 'Property of LGH in 3" letters on the back. However that was as nothing to the amount of stuff purloined, at every opportunity from the well endowed London Hospital Whitechapel (LHW)!
Cherub and his crew ended up assembling extra beds in 'P' and 'Q' Wards, with furious Sisters in General Medicine taking the overflow. Grace Laing was on the Wards with her sleeves rolled up day and night ensuring that every patient no matter how old or feeble got a standard of care I would have been happy for my own grandmother to have.

Chapter 13

Paediatric Nursing

The Paediatric Ward consisted of two sections, isolation cubicles and a main ward. There were eight cubicles, four on both sides of the ward nearest to the door, and the main ward was a mixture of cots and beds. Cots were extra large and were allocated to children up to the age of 5y while beds were allocated to older children. Each of the eight cubicles were self contained with glassed windows separating each one, there was a single cot and wash basin in each cubicle also a shelf for equipment, a Milton sterilizer and hooks for barrier gowns. You could bet your bottom dollar that you always remembered "just one more thing" you needed after you've gowned, gloved, and masked and gone into an isolation room. You could also guarantee your nose would itch the moment you gloved up. Likewise you forget what it was you wanted after you degowned and went to the supply cupboard. The word 'Barrier' nursing entered our vocabulary as we spend our day's gowning and ungowning between cubicles nursing children with croup, infectious diseases and gastroenteritis. Happy Campers (croups and whooping cough), usually admitted in a state of exhaustion between bouts of coughing were nursed in a steam tent within a cubicle. You could always tell a nurse looking after the 'Happy Campers' by her drooping hair and steamed complexion.

Spots, Dots and Squits included measles, meningitis, chickenpox, erysipelas and impetigo were our commonest contagious admissions and without broad spectrum antibiotics some of these children were very ill indeed. The poor babies with gastroenteritis were hooked up to drips and nursed in double

traction without nappies their bums slathered in Lassar's Paste to prevent excoriation of the buttocks.
Diphtherias' and Scarlet Fevers were transferred on to whatever Fever Hospital could find space for an 8-10 week stay, but in an outbreak Fever beds were in short supply. A rare complication in Scarlet Fever was a streptococcal infection affecting the kidneys. Kidney failure could occur as a consequence and the patient would die. In scarlet fever the children shed their skin like reptiles. The skin would peel off painlessly around the third week in quite large pieces which fascinated them. All desquamation had to be eradicated before they were discharged. The scarlet butterfly cheeks, the starkly contrasting white area around the nose and mouth, and the strawberry tongue and sandpapery rash were unmistakable in scarlet fever but were not always easy to differentiate in the early stages so children were admitted to await microbiology and pathology results or the outcome of a Dick's test which was a skin test like a tb test to determine susceptibility or immunity to scarlet fever. Diagnosis by a positive test took 8 to 24 hours.

The commonest cause of admission to the main ward up to the age of 5 years was for removal of tonsils and adenoids (T's & A's) closely followed by mastoiditis so a dozen or so cots/ beds were allocated to the Ear, Nose and Throat Team. Ear discharges were putrid so were swabbed with hydrogen peroxide daily, then mopped out with saline. A hated job but one I did willingly because it gave such relief to the children. Before antibiotics, mastoiditis was one of the leading causes of childhood deaths. Now it is a relatively uncommon and much less dangerous condition. Surgery to remove part of the bone and drain the mastoid was routine and drainage through the middle ear via the eardrum was often needed to treat pre disposing middle ear

infection. Complications included meningitis, facial palsy partial and total hearing loss.
By far the most troublesome children were the T's & A's. Fit and well on admission they were handed over at the Ward door. A menace before the operation, and like enraged demons after it because they weren't allowed visitors, they were best subdued with jelly and ice cream which they inevitably puked up all over themselves and us, usually just after you had put on a clean apron. You could consider yourself lucky if your stockings and shoes escaped. Kept in overnight in case of post-op haemorrhage we couldn't wait to discharge them and hand them back to their mothers the following morning.

Although fractures were the commonest cause for admission between 6-14y the older children were usually nursed on the adult Orthopaedic Ward strung up on traction to keep them out of mischief. Like the T & A's they were to be the bane of my life when I was allocated there.

The 1959 Mental Health Act ended the old asylum system responsibility for looking after people with epilepsy so children with 'fits' were now routinely admitted. A condition cloaked in mystery and fear was responding to new anti-epileptic drugs like carbamazepine and sodium valproate controlling seizures as never before so children were being admitted for assessment and control of symptoms. Identifiable by their fit charts and kidney bowl with tongue depressor, forceps and airway on their locker tops their behaviour ranged from hyper manic to underwater torpidity depending on how their medication was being fined tuned. It would be 1973 before Magnetic Resonance Imaging (MRI) was invented and developed for medical use to show us what was actually happening in the brains of these children.

To avoid cross infection, Sister Hart, alias 'The Duchess' allocated and rotated her students into 'Tents', 'Infectious' and

'General' which we interpreted as Happy Campers, Spots, Dots and Squits and Fits and Nits. We also did our stint in the Milk Kitchen where, remembering Eileen Williamson's scorn, I quickly made it my business to know what pathogens I was battling against.

Whatever the reason for a child's admission they were submitted to a bath, nit combing and painted a lurid purple or red on arrival. Nearly all the children were seriously grimy and bore some evidence of one infestation or another from lice, fleas, scabies, and ringworm to molloscum contageosum. Clothes were bagged and fumigated and all children dressed in hospital apparel.

On the ward the children's food was good although it lacked variety. It was mainly minced chicken, diced vegetables and boiled potatoes, with rice pudding for dessert or jelly for sickly children. In most cases this was better food than at home but this did not stop the children examining it with the greatest suspicion. Brought up on Kelly's Pie, 'mash and liquor', mushy peas, winkles and jellied eels, they looked on boiled potatoes, multicoloured vegetables and chicken in wonderment.

Posey Mc Donald, so dubbed because of her given name, Rosemary, as well as her pretentious affectations, was a sophisticate from Co. Limerick. She and I were scrutinising the Christmas off-duty rota. 'The Duchess', fed up with conflicting requests had washed her hands of the whole affair informing us that we could arrange to swop shifts with a counterpart from our own Set. Posey was mine. The Set had by now formed little groups who had similar interests so Posey was not somebody I hung around with, although she was one of the nurses who went to the Friday night dinners I attended, coming, escorted by her boyfriend Yusuf.

Swopping became quite contentious as I soon as I realised I was getting a raw deal. Sister had quite fairly tried to follow early shifts with late shifts to allow a sleep in if you had been out the evening before and she had given everybody a day off either Christmas Eve or Day, and the same for the New Year. I would have been quite happy to swop the entire rota with Posey because I didn't mind which days off I had, but when I found she had cherry picked the late and early shifts I ended up without a single lie in. She sulked for days, then cajoled, and when all else failed changed the rota hoping I wouldn't notice. Luckily I did and pointed it out to 'The Duchess' who had a carbon copy, but Posey, not to be outdone, failed to turn up for duty feigning illness on the first shift that didn't suit her. Sister felt duty bound to report a sick nurse to Bette and Joan, whom, I'm told were delighted to have a patient in the Infirmary over the holidays, especially one working on the Paediatric Ward who could be incubating any number of infections.

Christmas on the Ward was as jolly as we could make it within the restrictions of fears of cross infection and nursing very sick children. The biggest concession was allowing parents to visit their bemused traumatised children, who thinking they had been abandoned were now confronted by ghostly apparitions in white who wanted to clasp them to their bosoms. Local shopkeepers and benevolent societies were unstinting in ensuring that the children on the Ward and attending Paediatric Outpatients had at least one present each, the latter distributed at a tea party in the Clinic by a bow tie sporting, short, spruce Santa in a costume big enough to fit the rugby prop from the Orthopaedic team who was next in line to don it. Outpatients Clinics were christened 'God's Waiting Rooms' because it was where you waited for 'God' in the form of whatever eminent Consultant was in charge of your destiny.

Apart from his touchy-feely tendencies the Randy Dandy was actually a very knowledgeable and well thought of Paediatrician with a private practice in Wimpole Street. Venerated by 'The Duchess,' if she hadn't been a good Presbyterian, she would have had a craven image of him on a plinth. As it was, among the display of photographs of the Royal Family adorning her office wall, she had a photo of him receiving some kind of Award.

His Ward rounds were unbelievably chaotic because she insisted that bottle feeding and changing be postponed until the round had finished. Try explaining that to a screaming baby or a toddler with a nappy full of steaming diarrhoeal stools. The stupidity of it was *so* obvious to me as a student nurse about to embark on a second year of training that I couldn't believe that nobody considered the fact that happy contented children were so much easier to examine. The morning that the world stood still I was allocated the care of abandoned twins. About a month old the female, Daisy, was a pretty little baby having undergone a talipes repair and was absolutely no bother at all unlike her frog like brother. Freddie's skin was excoriated with eczema, he was a difficult feeder, was failing to thrive and had the most ear splitting heart rending cry I have ever heard in one so young. To get him sucking was a major achievement so I was ecstatic with delight watching the milk level steadily reducing in the bottle as the entourage swept past me to the next cot. 'The Duchess' gave me 'The Look' but what she didn't know was that in my nineteenth year of life I had survived more Killer looks than was good for me. To those who knew me well they knew you could hang, draw and quarter me and I would not be cowed into backing down. Words passed between her and Staff Nurse.

'Put Freddie back in his cot' Staff whispered to me.

'When he's finished' I responded with an uncompromising glare, thinking 'Jezzis, Grace Laing here I come'.

Deciding on a little 'Custody of the Eyes' at this point the next thing I was aware of was a neat pair of feet in silk socks and

handmade shoes, toe to toe with me, still seated and feeding Freddie.
'P-u-t t-h-e b-a-b-y *down* Nurse' a voice behind me ordered, but emulating Perseus I shunned the gaze of the Gorgon boring holes in the back of my head and turned to the Randy Dandy to have my say.
'Sir, if you'd like to examine Daisy first Freddie will be ready in a minute' I explained.
An amused pair of grey eyes gazed into mine and, with a wink, responded
'Splendid idea Nurse' and so within minutes a contented Freddie was back in his cot, fed, cleaned and changed.
'And how is this young man' said 'Sir' lifting the gurgling baby off the pillow propping him up and aeroplaning him above his head. To this day I contend that 'Sir' should have been aware that one of the reasons for Freddie's difficult feeding and failure to thrive was his lax gastric sphincter which enabled him to regurgitate at the slightest provocation, hence his propped up position. Declining to wear the customary white coat, four ounces of Half Fat National Dried Milk cascaded down the Randy Dandy's head and face to seep inside the collar of his Jermyn Street shirt and settle on the shoulders of his Saville Row suit. I believe curdled milk takes some getting out of worsted wool!
Before facing 'The Duchess' I had to endure an earful of wrath about the way I went about my stand from Eileen Williamson who was on the Ward clinically supervising a third year. (Murphy's Law strikes again!)
'Defying a Sister in public demeans not only her standing but the standing of other Sisters' she told me in cutting tones.
'It would obviously be sensible for Ward routine to continue during the round, but find a more circumspect way of dealing with the problem and I'm sure it can be resolved' she continued,

her glance implying expectation and an element of disappointment.

I took myself off to 'The Duchess's' Office to accept my fate. I don't remember much about our one-to-one but I didn't end up on Grace's carpet. My punishment was a week with the Happy Campers and floating in the Milk Kitchen. I don't know what transpired between Eileen Williamson and 'The Duchess' or whether the Randy Dandy had a hand in it, but the Ward ceased coming to a standstill during future rounds, so whatever the reason for the change of heart it was worth it. One of the most upsetting things about looking after the twins was not being allowed to follow their progress once they left the Ward. I had visions of them being returned to their feckless mother, being separated or ending up in Barnardo's or other long term care.

I thought this experience was far behind me when nearly a decade later I met the Randy Dandy in very different circumstances. I recognised him instantly and remembering his problem with spatial awareness I manoeuvred to ensure some personal space around me. It must have been his improving tennis expertise or becoming more mature that solved the problem because any discomfort around him seemed to be in the past. His furrowed brow and puzzled countenance as he tried to place me followed me around the room as I ensured everybody had food and drink.

'I know you from somewhere, but for the life of me I can't remember where' he said, exasperation turning to desperation.

'1958 – St. Andrew's Hospital Paediatric Ward – National Dried' were enough clues to light up his twinkling eyes.

'My God, the bolshi nurse' he exclaimed in amusement turning the heads of the assembled guests. He then regaled them with a highly embellished version of events ending with the information that he never managed to get the smell of putrid milk out of the jacket. Having been able to follow the twin's progress through his Out-Patient Clinic he was able to tell me that after tracing the mother who showed no disposition to wanting them back they were freed for adoption to a family in Kent, and that Freddie, recovering from his initial problems had become a handsome toddler before he was discharged from follow-up.

For more reasons than the current chronology allows this was heart warming news.

Chapter 14
Smoke Gets In Your Eyes.

The functions of the Endocrine System came too late in our training to allow me to apply a Neurologist's rationale to 'falling in love'.

They believe that three main neurotransmitters are involved in the attachment stage; adrenaline, dopamine and serotonin.

Clinically this stage of falling for someone activates your stress response, increasing your blood levels of adrenalin and cortisol and has the stupefying effect that when you unexpectedly bump into your new love, you start to sweat, your heart races and your mouth goes dry and you are struck dumb. With smoke filled eyes newly smitten lovers idealise their partner, magnify their virtues and explain away their flaws.

Having no intention of getting involved with 'boy friends' until I had completed my training social events crept up on me and before I knew it I had acquired a new group of friends of whom Minty was one. He met my boyfriend criteria at the time which was well polished shoes, clean nails, common sense and a good sense of humour.

He was intelligent, had a strong work ethic a competitive streak but an ability to lose gracefully. As well as his well polished shoes he was also clean, neat and good looking and I never once had to use my 'mad' money. What I didn't give enough consideration to as time went by was factors that help you form bonds and relate to each other, like having memories of the same things, such as the same historical, cultural and musical background. There's nothing worse than having to explain 'the craic' to somebody or have to apologise to for the deadly weapon that was Dublin wit and sarcasm, and although I was too immature to consider it then, someone you are sure has similar moral/ethical values and sense of justice.

Minty and I met at the 'India Club,' a restaurant on the second floor of the Strand Continental Hotel opposite Bush House in Alwych. Full of history the Hotel had a colonial-style décor but provided little more than hostel type accommodation to Indian Students arriving in London. Its second floor canteen was grandly called a restaurant. Its affordable prices and its South Indian food, which was served to perfection, made it a popular place to eat particularly for Bush House BBC staff and the Indian High Commission across the road.

I have no recollection of how the Friday night group started but I remember being invited to my first dinner by Leila who's boyfriend, Gideon, was a member of the group. Diners consisted of a group of South African Asian students converting their South African matriculation into acceptable grades required for English and Irish University entry, and student nurses sharing expenses to have a meal together. As nurses, shift rotas dictated our attendance, so my relationship with Minty started innocently enough with phone calls to check if I would be there or not. While this sounds like a simple task it was not a labour to be undertaken by the simple minded. Trying to contact one nurse among many in a Nurses Home with one public phone box was akin to a Herculean endeavour. We therefore ended up choreographing times to phone which began to imply a sort of commitment to meet up on Fridays.

During the 1950's there was a whole process to the 'going steady' ritual. With boys I had grown up with in Dublin we hung around in groups talking on street corners and later in Cafolla's Ice-cream Parlour sharing a Knickerbocker Glory or a Peach Melba. We would take it in turn to buy something on the menu or drink frothy coffee so that Antonio wouldn't throw us out for sitting listening to the Juke Box and flirting for an hour or so. Flirting was used to initiate the whole dating process so that any initial shyness could be eased away by the presence of others, but being brought up to participate in Dublineze repartee it was not a problem my friends and I experienced, however while we practiced a lot the process of dating seldom followed because it had financial consequences for the boys involved. To invite one of us out meant he was expected to pay for the honour. Girls at the time often insisted on double-dates both to placate their Mammies and Daddies and to indicate to the boy that he would be keeping his hands to himself. After double dating, you would naturally move onto single dating and the ubiquitous "going steady" or 'committed' stage. Engagement followed and many saw this stage as a kind of "play-marriage" for young couples. The exclusiveness of an engagement, sealed by a ring was taken as a promise of marriage but did not include 'trading a treasure for curiosity'. It would be another decade before The Pill would herald a change of attitude.

Dating had never been on my teenage agenda firstly because of the inordinate amount of homework the Nun's set us, being of the view that the Devil made work for idle minds and secondly my move to the other side of Dublin to do a year's pre nursing training, where again, the Nuns kept our hands and our brains busy and paid us so little that a Knickerbocker Glory at the end of the month became a luxury requiring due consideration.

Minty and I began dating when I was in Monolulu Land about eight months into my training. We progressed from India Club dinners to forming a foursome with Leila and Gideon to go occasionally to Lyon's Corner House for tea or the cinema or theatre. We also enjoyed the free entertainment that London provided such as going to Speakers Corner, Band Concerts in Hyde Park, or visiting museums. Cricket season saw Leila and me watch them play in far flung corners of Essex and Middlesex. The only excitement the latter provided was breaking London Transport regulations by travelling without tickets in the hope we could claim for a much shorter journey at our destination. Minty and Gideon and two of the other students in the group lived communally in Clapham and as it was a trek from East London it seemed the most natural thing in the world for Leila and I to stay over after an evening out to avoid the hassle of breaking curfew, or enduring Home Sisters interrogation if asking for a late pass. Getting in to a Nurses Home after lock-up has been variously described in other nurses memoires, suffice to say it was difficult, not at all amusing and on cold wet foggy nights was definitely not a desirable way to end to an evening.

While I grew up in a country riven by political differences and religious adherences on the other side of the world in Apartheid ridden South Africa Minty grew up in a country torn apart by racial differences. Prior to his arrival in London Minty had been raised in Klerksdorp, which as its name suggests, was Boer Country so was not conducive to inter-racial mixing. The expectation of his family would be for him to consent to an arranged marriage when he had qualified as a doctor.

The prospective bride would be Muslim and would have an unblemished reputation. Her ancestry and her family's culture and traditions would be important so they would look for a girl from families from the same region and having the same blood lines, language and food habits.

It would be expected that her family's assets would provide her with a dowry unless she was marrying beneath herself. Then Minty's professional qualifications would compensate for any inequality in family assets, and put a value on him as excellent husband material.

Quite apart from these hindrances, to continuing a relationship with the intention to marry the Parliament of South Africa prohibited, amongst other things, sexual relations between white people and people of other races. The Immorality Act, 1957 subsequently (renamed the Sexual Offences Act, 1957) repealed the 1927 and 1950 acts and replaced them with a clause prohibiting sexual intercourse or "immoral or indecent acts" between white people and anyone not white. It also increased the penalty to up to seven years imprisonment for both partners.

As far as my family was concerned Minty might be a 'Forner' and a heathen but at least he wasn't a protestant. In the process of applying for a place to study medicine at the Irish Royal College of Surgeons in Dublin he could be kept under surveillance if he was accepted. He was exotic enough for colour not to be an issue since Dublin was a city of learning so we were familiar with Asian and African students, but playing cricket put him beyond redemption. In a country answerable to God in the guise of DeValera and his all powerful Disciples in the GAA he might have got away with Soccer or Rugby, but cricket bore all the hallmarks of the West Brit Ascendency class which was used as pejorative term to suggest their continuing allegiance to the crown. Therefore Islam was not the important issue, the foot he dug with was. The question was;

'In his heart was he a Catlick or Prodisan?

Despite all the pressures to fool around, virginity was still a virtue in the fifties. For me after more than a year of dating, and two years into my training, matters got out of hand. Deep down I knew it was wrong, but left it too late to prevent the inevitable.

Chapter 15

Gynaecological Nursing

On return from a month's holiday in Ireland in February 1958 and absorbing news bulletins about the Munich disaster which had decimated the young Manchester Team I sat the State Prelims. The Exam was preceded by a week's block on Reproductive Health following which we would be allocated to either Obstetrics or the Gynaecology Ward. By far the most memorable lecture of the week was the one given by Grace Laing on Ethics and the Conscience Clause.

Conscience clauses are clauses in law and professional codes of practice which permit doctors, nurses and other providers of health care not to provide certain medical or nursing services which their moral or religious principles forbade them to participate in without being disciplined or discriminated against for refusing to do so. For Nurses to evoke the 'conscience clause' in the 'Professional Code of Conduct' we had to

'Make known to appropriate person or authority any conscientious objection which may be relevant to professional practice'.

In our case this came down to letting Sr. Williamson know whether we were prepared to accept an allocation to the Gynaecological Ward. Allocations were this Ward Sisters nightmare. If she was lucky she got willing volunteers. If she wasn't she had to ensure students did not participate in the nursing care post abortion. As far as I was concerned I was prepared to provide nursing care for these patients without jeopardising essential components of my own values. That did not mean I condoned or tolerated the terrible choice they had made. I also believed that judgement should be left to God, and if he was merciful, despite what the church taught, he would not throw them into the fiery furnaces of hell. When I put my name

on the list it was difficult to tell from Eileen Williamson's inscrutable expression whether she approved or disapproved.
The discussion was raised at a Catholic League of Nursed meeting the following evening when the Chaplin announced that we would be risking our immortal souls by nursing 'fallen women' and participating in giving them safe sex advice. So much for Mary Magdalene! I spoke my mind amidst frosty disapproval so was surprised to see two other RC names of members of my set, who hadn't uttered a word, on the allocation list when it went up. However my cards were marked by the Chaplin as I slid into apostasy. 'If you continue down this path you will not receive absolution which will mean you will not be in a state of grace to receive the sacraments'.
So be it.

Up to this point in training we had light heartedly called the Gynaecological Ward 'Saints and Sinners', but there was nothing light-hearted about the three months we spent there. The patients ranged from women in for investigations of infertility or facing threatened abortion of a much wanted baby to repair of prolapses. At the other end of the scale were the back street abortions (BSA's) and the self induced (DIY) abortions. Unlike other Wards where one had a sweeping view of 28 beds this Ward had a lot of pulled screens. Although this was my first allocation to a female ward I was aware from previous nursing experience that women patients were a gregarious bunch so the other noticeable thing on this ward was the women did not talk to each other and that the usual casual banter between beds was noticeably absent. Records were kept under lock and key in Sisters Office and meals were served at the bedside and not the communal table. 'What's she in for' was a common whispered enquiry as we went from patient to patient bed making or taking temperatures. Remembering Grace Laing's warnings of instant dismissal for any breach of confidentiality our lips were sealed. However on one occasion one of the 'infertility' patients was talking bitterly and loudly about criminals who kill babies while others struggle to get pregnant. I was aware that her difficulty conceiving was a result of cervical incompetence usually associated with previous abortions so was tempted to utter the words 'Glass houses' but made do with a knowing look which stopped her in mid sentence.

A woman's right to control her own body is taken for granted now, and today's nurses can scarcely believe that abortion used to be a criminal offence, punishable in law. Doctors, midwives and hospitals were required to report to the police if they suspected an abortion but I don't remember this ever happening. We all knew what the women on our Ward had suffered; prosecution would punish them and their family further. But for every woman we protected we also shielded the abortionist, whom most of us would have wished to see behind bars.

By refusing contraception to all but married women the law, church and society allowed abortionists to flourish. Chronic ill health frequently followed a BSA – endometriosis, bacterial infections, cystitis or nephritis, incontinence, a torn cervix or perforated colon were common. Fatalities among women who underwent abortions were high, but they were far higher among women who tried a DIY method. Knitting needles, crochet hooks, and other implements have all been pushed into the uterus by desperate women who preferred anything to the continued pregnancy. There have always been women who wanted or needed to end a pregnancy. Rich women would find a way, but for poor women it was a different story. With married women it was too many children - far more than they could house and feed decently, and for them another baby would be a disaster. I had yet to embark on a sexual relationship but I was well aware that for single women, illegitimate pregnancies meant social condemnation, banishment and economic disaster. For Catholics contraception was a sin, but there was a gray area around 'family spacing' that allowed the use of the safe period and abstinence. A woman with a regular menstrual cycle is usually able to get pregnant for about 5 days each month, when ovulation occurs. On average, ovulation occurs midway through the menstrual cycle. Because sperm can live for 3 to 5 days in a woman's reproductive tract, it is possible to become pregnant if intercourse occurs several days before ovulation so it is not an ideal solution as I was to find to my cost.

Thousands of women intent on an abortion tried some sort of medicinal way of evacuating the uterus from drinking quinine to taking advertised 'Cures for Menstrual Blockages' or sitting in steaming baths with bottles of Gin. I believe that the Turkish Baths in Bethnal Green was a popular locality for the latter. When all else failed, desperate women were driven to the backstreet abortionists.

The horrors of secret backstreet abortions are well documented elsewhere. Killing a foetus was done without anaesthetic, with unsterilized, obsolete or unsuitable surgical instruments, often on kitchen tables, by medically untrained people with no real knowledge of anatomy. Such abortions were agonizing and carried a high risk. Piercing the amniotic sack to rupture the membrane was specialty of some abortionists as was the use of Sea-tangle tents which were narrow tampons of the dried stem of the seaweed Laminaria digitata. They were used to dilate a woman's cervix to induce labour or an abortion, and purges with Epsom salts or soapy water were also universally used. Women died and the foetus survived.

Under the 1861 Offences against the Person Act, any person who 'unlawfully' used an instrument or any other means whatever to procure the miscarriage of a woman was considered to have committed a felony (a particularly serious crime in the same category as rape or murder). Therefore when a patient died as a result of such a procedure, they were not considered to have died during a medical operation so were not included in Maternal Mortality Rates but were recorded as a death as a result of 'violence'. A charge of murder could be brought against the person who carried out the procedure and a conviction could carry a death sentence.

Even the Artisans' Dwellings in Dublin where I had been reared did not escape the fatal outcome of an abortion by the infamous Irish abortionist, Mamie Cadden. A neighbour's sister, one of the brightest and the best, who was talented enough to be a dancer in the famous Olympia Theatre Dance Group was found dead, in the early hours of the morning, on the pavement in Hume St. where Cadden had her premises. I was only 13y at the time so had no idea what had happened, but was wildly curious about how she had been 'murdered'. But the Dwellings looked after its own, and while there might have been plenty of speculation behind closed doors and in the newspapers none of us children got to know the sordid details. It was only shortly before I came to St. Andrews, when Cadden was given a death sentence on Christmas Eve, for the death of another woman that I learned Bridget had also been a victim, dying from an air embolism following one of Cadden's procedures. As for Bridget, I can only think her reason for such desperate measures was that she thought a baby would have blighted her career but, in reality, her large warm-hearted family would certainly have been there for her and the baby.

My saddest day on the Gynae Ward was seeing five little children, the youngest still a babe in arms, being brought in by their costermonger father to say goodbye to their dying mother. Another abiding memory is of Grace Laing sitting by the bedside of seriously damaged women talking quietly to them. We knew she wasn't there on a ward round so Sister would nod to let us know to leave her in peace.

Chapter 16

Obstetric Nursing

Locally women clung to the traditions of their mothers and at least 50% of babies were born at home, many by gas light, in accommodation which had rotting floors, crumbling ceilings and damp seeping walls. In the old 'two up, two down' terraces two families often rented either the upstairs or downstairs sharing an outside privy and cold water tap. In the tenements water had to be carried up several flights of tenement stairs in houses still ravaged by the aftermath of the Blitz, and boiled up in the copper for the midwife's use. The conditions in which many women gave birth in the 50's meant high maternal and perinatal mortality rates, not only because of their grimly impoverished surroundings but because of what they were expected to endure with neither the means nor the knowledge to plan their families and prevent yearly pregnancies. With the Family Planning Service in its infancy and the Abortion Act still ten years hence Criminal Abortion aka BSA and botched DIY attempts was a leading cause of death associated with pregnancy and a high price to pay by both the pregnant women and their dependents. Family planning provision was not included in the National Health Services Act which established the NHS so 'Children by Choice not Chance' was still a decade away. The rhythm method or Standard Days Method estimate the likelihood of fertility based on the length of the users menstrual cycle was permitted by the Roman Catholic Church but required a degree of knowledge not available to local women if the local priests had their way. It also depended on the compliance of an understanding husband willing to avoid pregnancy by restricting sex to about eight days a month during his wife's least fertile period, abstaining from intercourse the rest of the time. Ten children or more being common it would appear that understanding husbands were an endangered species!

While it is now possible to get 'the morning after pill' or an abortion on the NHS eliminating the need for back street abortionist's, some women, e.g. illegal immigrants or girls at risk of family reprisal, who can't, or won't, use the services available, are fodder for fake herbal remedies and illegally obtained 'abortion' drugs. Fifty years on little has changed for some women.

An unwanted pregnancy was not the only consequence a woman had to worry about. A steady rise in the Wassermann reaction serum test, done routinely antenatally since WW2, despite false positives for Malaria and Tuberculosis, indicated a steady rise in syphilitic disease in women and was often the first indicator a woman had since there were often no symptoms to alert them. Syphilis was controllable, by penicillin and contact tracing but women who did not present for ante-natal care often escaped testing. Gonorrhoea, just as prevalent, was less amenable to treatment or diagnosis Smear testing was invasive so was only carried out if a test for syphilis was positive or a purulent vaginal discharge was detected at delivery, or post natally, when an infant was diagnosed with ophthalmia neonatorum, a gonorrhoeal eye infection which, before effective antibiotic treatment, could lead to blindness.

Even though prostitutes were encouraged to attend special VD clinics for health checkups they were offered no means of protection apart from periodic testing which gave them a false sense of security. They were however referred to Moral Welfare Officers for guidance back to the path of righteousness. For the wives of infected men, shame and embarrassment prevented them seeking post infection checks, and routine ante-natal smear cultures for gonorrhoea only became widespread in the late 1960s.

I hated Obstetrics and the little coterie of Sisters who ran the Maternity Unit. It was the one Department that did not have its own personal God. Yes, there was a Consultant, or two, but this was the realm of Queen Bees in fierce competition in the Ante Natal Beds, Labour Rooms and Post Natal Ward. With Student Midwives and Medical Students vying for deliveries we poor student nurses had a hard job signing off on the six births we were supposed to observe. We were chivvied from pillar to post fetching and carrying, bowing and scraping, standing to attention to anything that moved, and scrubbing or autoclaving anything that didn't. Observing the miracle of birth did not make up for the hours of drudgery we endured.

The 50% of women who chose a hospital delivery availed themselves of a high standard of aseptic care, the availability of new drugs such as oxytocin, sulphonamides & penicillin, as well as improved blood transfusions, all of which lead to a decline in maternal deaths of 400 per 100.000 live births in 1940 to 30 deaths per 100,000 live births in 1959. However the Labour Ward was not a place for discussing ante-natal choices with mothers-to-be. Women in labour ranged from the stoical to the maniacal and even tho' I was born and reared in working class Dublin I learned some choice new words to add to my vocabulary. These words were aimed at their impregnators whose presence during labour was not encouraged, and who dealt with their exclusion by pacing the main corridor with haggard beseeching expressions, however, the majority handed over the phone number of the nearest hostelry as they repaired to its comfort and the sympathetic company of its clientele to await the outcome.

I don't doubt that the women got good care, and a lot of them had their babies in the safety of St. Andrew's from choice. I think this had more to do with the 10 day 'Lying In' period offered post natally which most newly delivered mothers regarded as a holiday, but whom many had to forgo because of family commitments, than the regimented rules they had to tolerate. In a hospital serving the working classes epidurals were unheard of, caesareans only performed as a last resort, pethidine used sparingly and progress was monitored with nothing more sophisticated than good record keeping, skilled palpation and a Pinard stethoscope (a trumpet-shaped device, put on the mother's abdomen while the midwife or obstetrician listens at the other end). Women laboured on their backs, legs in stirrups, sucking gas and air until the tank rattled. Following birth the babies were removed to the Nursery to be returned to their mothers for four hourly feeding. This was perfectly acceptable practice at the time in the belief that a baby established in a routine would be a happy thriving baby, but while the mothers submitted to it, it was a common sight to find some of them weeping and lactating at the Nursery viewing window gazing on their bawling angry offspring, gobs wide open as their rooting reflexes sought something to suck. Looking at this scene it was plain to see why the Unit deserved the sobriquet 'Obs and Gobs'. I had no idea how mothers could tell the squalling bundles of fury apart but each mother seemed to have a built in frequency device that allowed them to hone in on the screaming despair of their own offspring.

Mothers with a fistful of kids already knew that four hourly routines did not work so would revert to prop feeding as soon as she got the new baby home resulting in a contented baby and a hands free mother. Explaining the dangers of prop feeding always evoked the response 'Well it didn't do me other kids no 'arm', usually reinforced by the grandma shoving her two ha'penny worth in with a 'Mine neither'.

Having nursed the prop feeders in Paediatrics I was well aware of the associated inhalation pneumonia, gastroenteritis, poor development of gross motor skills and even death from hypernatremia, and therefore knew that some of these babies would be showing up on our morbidity statistics, but hopefully not on our mortality figures.

Regardless of the fact that I had already found a dead body in a ward toilet during my St. Anne days my second one was a much greater shock because there was a 36 week old foetus inside her who might still have a chance to live.

Mavis, a sturdy, resilient woman, the mother of two boisterous boys and the wife of a 'barrow boy' who knew his place in the scheme of things, had been on strict bed rest for nearly four weeks suffering from pre eclampsia. A reluctant patient she was under constant watch and monitoring awaiting a caesarean as soon as the foetus was mature enough to survive. Finding her bed empty I went looking for her to be met by another patient panting with fright telling me Mavis was on the toilet floor having a fit. Sending her on her way to find a Sister I ran into the Toilets to discover Mavis in an inert heap on the floor.

'Was she dead'?

I didn't know, but as I felt her stomach I knew the baby wasn't. I also knew that there was very little time to attempt to extract it. In days before 'Crash Teams' getting access to emergency help was a hit and miss affair. It seemed like eternity before Sister arrived. I know it had been too long for me to stand by and do nothing so I had set off the Fire Alarm.

Looking out the window overlooking the rear of the hospital seeing The Don preparing for evacuation of the entire Maternity Unit I have to admit in retrospect that it was not a rational decision, and caused untold chaos, however it did bring people running to the scene resulting in giving the baby a fighting chance of survival. Removing a baby is a crude affair. Once the mother is pronounced dead the length of the abdomen is opened with the nearest sharp instrument and the baby extracted and resuscitated. Mavis's little girl had been deprived of oxygen for too long so did not survive.

I learned to live with the notoriety of allegedly calling out the Fire Brigade to deliver a baby in a Maternity Unit for the rest of my training. Whenever I sought advice about solving a problem I would be greeted by the sarcastic response 'Why don't you call the Fire Brigade'? Little did the mockers know but I had committed a greater sin than *that,* which I hoped would never reach the ears of Sr. Josephine. I had not said the Prayer for the Dying over Mavis's departing soul.

Considering the circumstances I'm sure God would have taken her straight to heaven but I know that that would not cut the mustard with Sr. Josephine.

Chapter 17

Chronic Medical

Moving from Maternity to Chroni Bronies on 'P' and 'Q' Wards was a joy. My allocation was to be split between the Female and Male Wards, the latter on nights. It was perhaps unfair to label all the patients as Chronic Bronchitics but Geriatric Medicine was not yet a recognised concept, so beds appeared to have been filled on the premise that Monolulu Land was for acute medical conditions while 'P' and 'Q' Wards beds were allocated to chronic conditions or welfare assessments, covering the age range from retirement to the grave. We had the same Juju Men, but none of the hassle of Intake and Output Charts or finicky diets so if patients wanted to indulge themselves on Jellied Eels, Whelks or Pie and Mash they had earned the right to do so.

My first day on the Ward and I thought I was back with the Happy Campers. Four bed bound women in oxygen tents was the first thing that caught my eye.

'Asthma, emphysema, lung cancer and chronic bronchitis' I learned from Sr. Noone's report.

'Full nursing care' she told us, and 'No smoking' she said firmly bringing to mind Seamus Hickey a patient at St. Anne's nicknamed the Widow Maker by the other men because he seemed intent on blowing up the Ward by smoking in his oxygen tent.

It was on the Chroni Bronies Wards that I first came into contact with East Enders of an age to have survived the trenches of WW1, struggled through the Great Depression and the devastation of WW2. Prematurely aged and gnarled their resilience and resourcefulness never ceased to amaze me, and their humour and appreciation of our care made our long hours easier. At that time we were working 48 hour weeks. Our patients sometimes stayed in for weeks so between the long hours of bedside care and lengthy bed occupancy we really got to know them and their families. This was not only a great privilege for us but a comfort to them. Despite the fact that we were used to seeing notices in Boarding House windows proclaiming 'Rooms to Let' with a supplementary notice stipulating No Irish, No Coloured, No Children, No Dogs I came to the conclusion that Landladies, like rapacious slum landlords were a breed apart because I never came across discrimination from an ordinary East Ender. The mere fact of looking at multinational family mixtures and neighbourliness gave a truer picture. The end of WW 2 had seen a marked increase in Caribbean migrants to Britain. However very few of them fancied a life on the docks so had not settled in Tower Hamlets, therefore, although Poplar had its quota of white working-class "Teddy Boys" the Notting Hill Riots in West London, as far as our Chroni Bronies were concerned, might as well be happening in Johannesburg, and the fuss about integration more commensurate with Little Rock or the far side of the moon. Although the National Front used to target Brick Lane, marching through the area on Sundays, the fascist marchers elicited little support from outside their own membership.

Any 'race riots' in the East End were long past and had been a result of dockers returned from the trenches after WW1 to find immigrants had filled their shoes by undercutting their wages. In the 1920's with a colour bar in place, supported by the Union, immigrant seamen lost their fight for parity of pay, so found they worked alongside white dockers for less money. Finding the guarantee of work reduced to daily battles they moved on to road building and construction necessitating moving to areas nearer to their source of employment. Seeing Commonwealth subjects fighting shoulder to shoulder with home grown recruits during WW2 dispelled a lot of stereotyping and aided acceptance.

During my weeks on the Ward I learned a whole new language describing anatomy and bodily functions and leave you to work out your own interpretations;

Anatomical representations in Cockney speak included Barnet Fair; Boat Race; Bread and Cheese; Bristol City, Farmer Giles; Cobbler's awls; Hampton Wick; Hobson's choice; Khyber Pass; Mince Pies; Mutt and Jeff, North and South; Oliver twist; Plates of meat and Loaf of bread.

Functions were identified as having a Jimmy Riddle; Pony and trap; Raspberry tart or a Turkish delight. Feeling 'Tom and Dick' brought one running with a vomit bowl and 'Brown bread' described the finality of it all.

Our Yiddish also improved but was mostly lamentational or sarcastic since hospital admission was enviably regarded as a *tsuris,* implying serious trouble.

'Oy vey iz mir' covered a multitude of situations expressing dismay, exasperation and grief while 'Oy gevalt' was reserved for shock horror. Feh! Which sounded like an Irish 'Feck' was an expression of disgust or disapproval reserved for the Kosher food served up for dinner, and 'Mazel Tov' was usually used ironically meaning 'it's about time' when one of us responded to a call for a bed pan. I was surprised to find that I knew a lot of the 's' words from the vernacular used in the working class areas of Dublin. Shalom, schlock, schmuck, shlep, shlimazel, shmaltz, shmooze, and spiel being a few. My favourite Yiddish expression was the humorous response to a 'Bowels open' enquiry.

A disgusted 'Bupkes' was the usual reply.

Coinciding with my swap over to nights on Chroni Broni Males were some of the worst pea soupers of the decade which that year came hand in hand with a major influenza epidemic. Asian 'flu appeared in the east in 1957 and spread as a pandemic to the UK. Treatment was purely symptomatic so the old, vulnerable, and those with chronic chest conditions were on the Ferryman's list. Bette and Joan were in their element with an Infirmary full of Nurses, which meant staff fit for duty was spread thinly while patient numbers increased exponentially creating crisis conditions. Routine admissions were suspended. Normally, at night, there would be a third and first year Nurse on the Chroni Ward under the guidance of Night Sister, Sr. Starr, who covered several wards. Still in my second year I found myself in charge of the Male Chroni's, with Mc Intyre, one of the clumsiest, stupidest first years I had ever come across in my life under my command. A klutz and shlimazel described her to a tee but an Irish 'Amadan' was sufficient to address my ire. She could not to be trusted with any task however simple so she doubled my workload.

Nursing assignments for the night were already overwhelming with six extra beds crammed into the Ward and at least ten patients in oxygen tents. If lives on the Ward were saved during this critical period it was down to Elvis, one of the most annoying Porters on 'The Don's' staff. Usually on day duty he had been transferred to nights to service our oxygen needs. In days before piped oxygen each patient, needing oxygen, had an individual tank and those in oxygen tents were eating it up. With no disarray to his Elvis quiff or scuffing to his blue suede shoes he not only zoomed around replenishing tanks but rearranged pillows, supplying urinals, made tea and stopped The Widow Makers lighting up. I learned that, with a few hours sleep he was back working on day duty and kept this up until the worst of the epidemic was over. All the hospital staff, including Dodger, Noddy and Gene Kelly worked like Trojans and Red Jack forgot about trade demarcation lines, but Elvis's contribution was memorable because normally he was such a divvy that my expectations of him were low. It taught me never to judge a book by its cover. My one regret is that I can no longer remember the name he was given at baptism, so Elvis if you are reading this your great contribution *is* remembered.

As for Mc Intyre, well if you've ever read stories about gormless nurses who do such unlikely things that nobody in their right mind would believe their exploits you need to meet this girl from the County Armagh. When I thought I had seen the utmost of her stupidity she never ceased to amaze me by going one step further. A few of her priceless moments were;

Putting all the patients' dentures into one bowl to clean them

Trying to connect a nasogastric milk feed to an intravenous saline drip

Informing me that a patient, behind drawn screens, whom I had sat with as he had slipped peacefully away, wasn't looking too well under the sheet covering his face as I waited respectfully for his soul to depart before laying him out.

And finally; replacing an oxygen cylinder with a gas and air cylinder. Luckily the patient was too weak to suck in the required amount of mixture to make him as high as a kite, but it didn't do his oxygen levels much good. A few months later I couldn't believe my eyes when I saw her name on the list proclaiming that she had succeeded in the State Prelims which I had sweated blood to pass.

Chapter 18

Mental Health Nursing; Beyond Barking

With no Psychiatric Wards at St. Andrews the secondment to Warley Mental Hospital in Essex for Psychiatric experience was viewed with mixed feelings by those of us who found ourselves on the allocation list. Our little group consisted of Margaret Mc Millan, Marion Smythe, Rhoda Dedrick and me. Lurid stories about lobotomies, padded cells and wards full of psychopaths being incarcerated behind its walls where foremost in my mind as I got ready to go 'It's a doodle' we were told by those who had already been. Used to the Monastic Asylum style of St. Andrews, Warley's, high Transylvania Gothic edifice was no surprise. However the size of the hospital site which housed 1600 long term patients was vast, stretching from the lodge on Warley Hill all the way down to Crescent Road and the railway line – a total area of almost 100 acres enclosed behind a wall capable of keeping the world out and safely containing patients and staff alike.

The Wards at Warley were all of uniform design consisting of single rooms, dormitories and day rooms. They opened off wide corridors, which were intended as a recreational space in bad weather. The latter space could only be used for walking up and down. It contained no chairs because of the patient's propensity to use them as weapons although those who had an interest in watching the parade often dragged armchairs from the Dayroom. They were very territorial of their space and a patient from another ward perhaps just bumming a cigarette could be set upon with little provocation. A lot of them were like old lags when it came to smoking. Their addiction had them hunting for discarded butts from which they would extract the last remnants of tobacco, in non filtered days, and save them until they had sufficient to hand roll a smoke.

Like St. Andrews the wards could be accessed by a series of cloister corridors but my recollection is that those at Warley were all enclosed. The Dayrooms were where the patients would sit and also have their meals. There were plenty of armchairs to sit on if they just wanted to gaze into the abyss or at the television screen which was always on, but muted, the BBC Interludes like an animated fish tank. Our reason for being there was to make sure they came to no harm and to keep them engaged. We wore a modified uniform, dresses but no aprons or caps and used to play card games, snakes and ladders, in fact any game that did not require too much concentration. As students we were never supposed to be left alone with the patients but the Warley Attendants were adept at creeping away for a crafty fag or a surreptitious cuppa. We were issued with a whistle to summon help but I never expected to use it. When I did it was nearly the death of me! Two of the gentlest most compliant elderly female patients started arguing over a card in Happy Families. When I tried to jolly them out of it one of them raised her chair and hit the other one over the head with it. Realising I was alone I should have blown the whistle; instead I decided to try to cajole the chair wielder into putting the chair down. She actually did but in a split second her victim lunged at me and grabbed the whistle chain around my neck and tried to strangle me with it. The only thing that saved me was the assailant crashing the chair down on top of her again. At which point I didn't have enough puff to blow it. Before I could even get up off the floor the two of them were back at the table continuing their game agreeing that Miss Doom the Undertakers Daughter should be conceded to the one who had the rest of the family e.g. my attacker. The only evidence that anything had taken place was my unpinned hair and the red weal around my neck.

However my most vivid memory of Warley was the lurid vermilion lino. There was miles and miles of it. It was probably chosen to give cosy feeling to vast spaces but it was so reminiscent of shiny rivers of blood it gave me panic attacks, so God alone only knows what effect it had on agitated patients playing Happy Families!

Our secondment covered experience in various Wards and took in Lunatics, Idiots, Imbeciles, Epileptics, and Catatonics. My memory of the Wards was the lack of individual space in the Imbecile sectors which had up to about 50 beds in them. Ever afterwards I only had to smell Paraldehyde to evoke memories of Warley. Paraldehyde, like Formaldehyde is a smell a nurse instantly recognises. It was introduced into clinical practice in the UK in 1882. A central nervous system depressant it was used as an effective anticonvulsant, hypnotic and sedative. In other words a magic elixir, and was commonly used to induce sleep in psychiatric hospitals and geriatric wards up to the 1960s. About 30% of the dose is excreted via the lungs which was the source of its unpleasant acetic acid smell that contributed to its strong odour on the breath of patients.

Warley, being designated as a long stay hospital, with few allocated medical staff, and with custody and storage as its main remit, there was little treatment available on site. Psychotherapy was in its infancy, and physical treatments, which included the use of chlorpromazine, insulin and electroconvulsive therapy, while available, were concentrated on acute patients in newer therapeutic Essex Psychiatric Hospitals. On the other hand the notion of Warley as an asylum, or a place of refuge and safety was well established and was seen as something that was needed by so many poor unfortunates secure in their institutionalization.

However there was a price to be paid for this. Patients were 'inmates' with no past and no future. Before the 1959 Mental Health Act, in the community of the insane, many of the patients had no legal or personal identity, not even a surname, or clothes of their own to wear. They had a bed to sleep in, and if they were sensible enough, a locker for their meagre possessions. Handbags were muched prized by the women but contained little apart from a comb and a grubby hanky, and were often confiscated after handbag fights! With the men it was their little baccy tins.

Despite the anxieties and complaints about conditions for patients in mental hospitals, many people were concerned at the prospect of closing the hospitals and requiring their patients to live in the community. The pros and cons of both systems have long been debated with very little space being given to patient choice or preference.

At Warley able-bodied patients were encouraged to work daily in the hospital grounds and buildings. This physical activity gave them stimulation and relief from boredom, and also provided the underfunded facilities with a large labour pool for basic maintenance. They also learned skills that were put to good use. Some of them worked on their own Ward helping less able patients and developed lasting loyalties and had lived at Warley for decades they regarded it as their home. Most jobs were sexually segregated to prevent the complications of relationships; the male patients tended the extensive grounds and worked in the bakery while the women did a lot of the cooking, cleaning, laundry and ironing. The latter also learned to sew and patch. The Occupational Therapy Departments, always short of funding did wonders with Sales of Work and teaching basket making and weaving skills. As well as Dayroom activities we took the 'Imbeciles' out for walks in the grounds. To call people 'Imbeciles' or 'Mental Defectives' now seems appalling, but was commonly used back then even for Census returns. These dreadful names covered categories of patients from the microcephalic 'Idiots' to adults with Down's syndrome or 'Mongols' and was meeting with professional disapproval by the 50's as were vernacular terms such as nut cases, fruit cakes, mental, lunatic, screwy or barking mad. The latter term was based on local train station names to indicate a degree of madness and was used euphemistically as 'Dagenham' or' TSBB' (Three Stops beyond Barking) which described severely disturbed patients.

On fine days we took 'the imbeciles' in the grounds for walks. In part of the gardens was a large old burial ground and patients loved the serenity of the graveyard section with its wildflowers, trees and the headstones of the patients and staff who were buried there. On one of my 'not engaging my brain days' I decided to teach a few of them how to play 'Hide and Seek'. 'Go and hide and be very quiet until we find you' I told the little group who scattered. 'The last one to be found wins the game'.

With the two who didn't understand I kept hold of their hands as we set out to find the hiders. Giggling and rustling made the job easy and amidst much cajoling of 'Again, Again' we played on. It was then I realised that Harold hadn't been found first time around. My heart froze in panic as I called and called with no reply. I blew my whistle which upset some of the group because it usually meant that somebody had been naughty, but as for any help forthcoming we might as well be out on the plains of the Serengeti. Common sense told me that Harold had not done a runner. A man in his 40's with Down's syndrome he thrived on the routine at Warley. I took the others back to the Ward and told the Charge Nurse I had lost Harold.

'Well go and find him' he told me brutally reminding me of my Aunt May the day we lost her young daughter, Winnie, in a similar game of Hide and Seek. I had told the biddable child to hide until she was found which is exactly what she did. A call to tea interrupted the game and it was only her empty chair that alerted us to her absence. We discovered the poor mite asleep in the hen house still waiting to be 'found'. And so it proved with Harold whom I discovered sitting on the branch of a monumental oak tree nearby.

'Didn't you hear me calling you' I asked in exasperation?

'Yes' he responded beaming, my exasperation lost on him.

'Why didn't you answer?

'Because you told me to be very quiet until you found me, he told me

'And you didn't find me'.

What could I say in the face of such logic?

'Did I win' he asked looking at me hopefully.

'Yes, Harold you're a champion' I told him, meaning it. His honest simplicity was heart warming and I wondered what family misfortune had put him in Warley for life.

As well as escorting little groups on walks patients were taken on charabanc outings to Southend and had a yearly Sports Day. Social life very much depended on the interest and enthusiasm of Ward Staff and reflected how a ward was led. Some Sisters / Charge Nurses saw themselves as little more than custodians, while others dedicated themselves to wellbeing of their charges working more hours than they were ever paid for. The custodian attitude was also mirrored in the manner of some Ward Attendants who felt they had a job for life with nobody to gainsay them but during my secondment I found the latter to be in the minority. The only activity I hated during my time there were the 'socials'. Knowing the patients enjoyed them I was introduced to the delights of barn dancing and waltzing. I endured trodden toes, clammy hands and paraldehyde halitosis but my tolerance did not encompass the clinches of some of the seedier Ward Attendants who deliberately changed the music to slow smooches to have the opportunity of clasping seconded students in their nicotine smelling embrace. An 'accidental' hard kick in the shins soon cooled their enthusiasm.

What did I learn at Warley? Well not a lot about the treatment of mental illness. That was left to Mr. George's tutorials on our return. I did learn it was difficult to tell patients and staff apart. Taking a gardening patient firmly in tow one evening he came meekly enough as I escorted him back to his Ward. I knew there was something amiss when the Charge Nurse jumped to attention when I ushered in the 'patient', Dr. Nightingale the Medical Director. I believe the Doc dined out on the story for sometime afterward.

I also learned there was there was a whole world behind asylum walls hidden from everyday life and that that world had little or nothing to do with headline grabbing stories about mad axe men, serial killers and other sociopaths and psychopaths locked up for life. Warley had no Forensic Unit so only hid our collective shame in locking up family members and vulnerable people, including children, we wanted to keep hidden. They were more risk to themselves than they were to us. I also learned there were no easy answers when it came to finding solutions. It also made me realise how little I knew about my own Aunt Alice cloistered in a Dublin Workhouse.

Chapter 19

Casualty

I loved Casualty from the first day I set foot in it. The lack of Ward routine was liberating. No bed making, bedpan rounds, medicine rounds, serving meals or keeping out of Sisters way. The day normally started with an empty department having seen the overnight shelterers on their way with an early cup of tea and a letter to a Local Refuge. The latter were a bone of contention between The Don and Grace Laing. His porters acted as security in Casualty when a patient got obstreperous or rowdy so he felt he should have some say in who sat in the Waiting Room on cold inclement nights. The occasional 'tramp' who just dozed the night away by a radiator was no trouble to us, but upset The Dons sense of order. Helping them on their way before he came on duty was in everybody's interest.

Casualty was as familiar to the local population as Woolworth's. We dealt with everything from children poking foreign objects into orifices to foreigners looking the wrong way at traffic lights and ending up under the wheels of a 25 bus. Every day we learned something new as we developed our observational skills and plastering and bandaging techniques. We vied with medical students to perfect our stitching expertise on our weekend semi-comatose drunks securely strapped to a trolley. There was no such thing as 'informed consent', if a drunk was on a trolley consent was 'implied' and we bribed children with lollipops without a thought for their dental health. We learned that children were braver than parents and that a great many people were stoical to the verge of insanity walking in with broken or severed limbs or bordering, on the verge of a cardiac arrest. Applying Murphy's Law we also learned that the first people in line when Casualty day shift started would not require urgent care but that a haemorrhaging workman or pending heart attack would walk in 5 minutes before your shift ended to collapse at your feet not having bothered to call an ambulance. We also observed that ambulances like buses preferred to travel in convoy!

Work at the docks was heavy, dirty and dangerous, and few dockers escaped injury. The frequent crush, winching and laceration mishaps, which had previously been treated at The Poplar Hospital for Accidents now had to be taken the considerable life threatening distance to the London Hospital, the rest were blue belled to us.

Ambulance cases normally got priority attention so when a trolley came through the sighs of the mass of walking wounded were audible when their waiting line came to a halt. Ambulances also created much needed diversion and discussion about the usually oblivious unfortunate occupant of the trolley. There was much to be said for the open plan Casualty Department of the old hospitals which allowed patients to see what is going on. I discovered this years later when I worked in a state of the art Accident Emergency Department which had a separate entrance for admission by ambulance out of sight of the walking wounded. The waiting room queue would remain static and a flashing neon clock with a waiting time that was constantly revised upwards just made patients see red. It didn't help that they were Hampsteadites and knew their rights!

It was in Casualty that I learned there was something I couldn't cope with. Up to now I had dealt with bodily fluids of every colour and description coming out of every orifice you can think of, but a warm evening in the Casualty Waiting Room I met my Waterloo and found I was defeated by a small squirmy mob waiting for me in a cubicle. A none too clean elderly gentleman was sitting on a chair with a bandaged foot in a slipper on an adjustable footrest.

'Can you take a look at my foot Nurse, he asked
'I think there's something not right with it, it feels numb' he added as I removed the bandage.
The sweet putrid smell of gangrene wafted up as the last turn of the bandage disclosed a greenish soaked piece of gamgee. Removing the gamgee with a forceps I was faced with two black toes and a purpling area extending down the metatarsals. A brief history elicited the fact that the District Nurse had bandaged his foot some days before, that he was a diabetic, and was on the list for an amputation. Cleaning up the foot before calling the Casualty Officer to take a look I bent the toes forward to clean behind them to discover that the ball of the foot had caved in and was now filled with hundreds of active fat white maggots. Unable to control my gag reflex I found myself vomiting into a soiled laundry basket being pushed by Red Jack as I cannoned into it on a rapid exit from the cubicle. Trying to ignore the row of astonished patients in the waiting room and Jack berating me I went back in the cubicle as if nothing has happened. Luckily the patient was still unaware of his cargo and of my reaction. A progression from Casualty Officer to Senior Surgical Houseman to Surgical Registrar resulted in the patient's admission, maggots and all.
'Re-bandage the foot Nurse' the Reg told me.
'Those maggots will do a grand job eating the dead flesh until we're ready to operate'.
It was some considerable time before I ate rice pudding again.
My most memorable day in Casualty was the morning I diagnosed Leprosy. Having attended a good Catholic school run The Daughters of Charity of St. Vincent de Paul I gave a tithe of my pocket money to feed little black babies in our far flung Irish Missions, and because we were more fortunate than others Father Damian's Lepers out in Surinam also had a claim on our

compassion. I acquired enough knowledge of Leprosy from watching our yearly viewing of 'The Leper Priest' to be able to diagnose it in a Lascar cook from a merchant ship who came in with a burned hand. The loss of feeling in both hands and silvery patches on his trunk confirmed it for me, but I was only a student nurse so a scathing Registrar sent off skin samples to prove me wrong. The Nuns would have been proud of me, I knew my Hansen's disease when I saw it!

Road traffic accidents we dealt with at the time occurred on urban roads. Pedestrians were the main victims while on country roads it was motorcyclists. The opening of the M1 motorway in 1959 led to a new style of driving and a new pattern of serious injuries. On the motorway the vast majority of patients were occupants of cars so a tiered system was proposed as guidance for the Ambulance Service resulting in identifying our life saving central accident unit as The London Teaching Hospital and St. Andrews as a District accident unit with support from peripheral casualty services at smaller Hospitals in our three boroughs.

Our saddest fatalities and most upsetting incidents were suicides. Taking a running jump under the Tube at Bow Road Underground Station was a regular occurrence. St. Clements Mental Hospital being less than a hundred yards from the entrance made it a popular spot. Attempters who were still alive were rushed to The London; the Succeeders were brought to us to be pronounced dead without ever leaving the ambulance. We all took our turn accompanying the Casualty Officer out to the Ambulance Bay on this usually solemn occurrence. The ambulance crew and I stood by as a cursory examination was made and a policeman checked for identification. This suicide was a man in his early forties. Strapped to an ambulance trolley the covering blanket was unfurled and he was superficially examined and declared dead. His clothes, stained with blood and smelling

of the soot and dirt from the tracks were a contrast to his face which was pale, peaceful and unmarked. However, as my eye travelled up and down the body there was something decidedly odd about it. It took me some time to realise what it was.
'His boots are on the wrong feet' I said to the small silent group. All eyes turned to the feet.
The Casualty Officer grasped one of the boots by the heel and came away with a below knee amputated leg cozily ensconced in it. A stomach lurching moment followed, succeeded by a mixture of profanity from all present that turned to hysterical laughter on my part when the realization hit me that the other leg must be in a similar condition. Inappropriate humour was our way of coping with exposure to death and brought back vivid memories of my maternal grandmother's funeral. Her last journey in her coffin from her bogside home to the village church was an occasion when I had behaved equally inappropriately. On this occasion there was no Mammy to slap me.

Chapter 20

Orthopaedic Nursing

Orthopaedic Wards grew out of former Crippled Children's Hospitals and Adult Rehabilitation Centres. The former treated children suffering from tuberculosis, osteomyelitis and poliomyelitis but thanks to Bacillus Calmette-Guérin (BCG), antibiotics and the polio vaccines the 'sunshine cure' was abandoned, to vanish almost entirely by the late 50's. The latter centres, amalgamated into the National Health Service, joined Crippled Children and specialist post war centres for amputee rehabilitation services and prosthetic provision. The increasing traffic on the roads and industrial accidents had given rise to accident cases requiring orthopaedic surgery, so District Hospital's became involved in the treatment of adults, which led to the opening of Orthopaedic Wards. It was an uneasy association until the advent of the thalamide disaster when limbless babies cemented their allegiance, and that of the Physiotherapy Department. While it was still possible to do two year training as an Orthopaedic Nurse our allocated time on the Ward was part of our General Training and did not count towards any specialization.

Big Bertha, Ward Sister on 'Sankey's, the Male Orthopaedic Ward was a force to be reckoned with. Although named after a Howitzer Tank she was a fine figure of a woman. She was tall, big boned, well muscled, rosy cheeked and had nice regular features. In comparison to the male Neanderthal Rugby types, known as Knuckle Draggers who were intent on following a career in Orthopaedic Surgery she was a Boadicean Goddess. She was also a very capable and hardworking Ward Sister who could singlehandedly lift a hefty patient from supine to a three pillow upright position with effortless ease. She was also the only ward sister who never rolled her sleeves down to put on her cuffs unless she was going to the dining room or off duty. Orthopaedic Wards were 'heavy wards' because of the amount of patients in traction. They were also 'difficult wards' because although most of the patients were bed bound they were otherwise young, fit and well, and capable of mischief.

If, like me, you are cursed from birth you would not be surprised to discover that one of your allocated patients is a 'patient from hell', a whiny 20 stone man in traction needing full nursing care, while my colleague, Myrtle Wilson's 'patient from hell', was an 8 stone Jack- the -Lad flyweight whose traction did not prevent him from swinging from the hoist like an orang-utan, nor did it impede in any way his groping expertise. More than half the ward were on traction so pressure area care was top priority and woe betides you if your patient had as much as a red mark over any bony prominence. Regular bowel movements were equally important and hard to achieve in bedbound patients. If simple aperients and pushing fluids didn't work, glycerine suppositories were tried, escalating to enemas, or the dreaded manual evacuation, which should have rightly been called an excavation since that was what it actually was. The danger with the latter was that it was like taking a cork out of a bottle when you explored the rectum with two gloved fingers to clear the impaction. Getting a heavy patient in traction onto a bedpan to disgorge a river of backed up brown slurry was usually, in my experience, doomed to failure unless Big Bertha was on hand. I could also guarantee that after changing the sheets the patient would has a residual purge and that the amount of clean bed linen available would be inversely proportional to the ward's immediate needs.

Groping the Nurses was a well tried pastime but Big Bertha was a past master at circumventing it. From cold bed baths to shaming them in front of their girlfriends, wives and mothers she was a woman without mercy. Fear of the reprobation of their matriarchal East End mothers was the greatest deterrent. To witness it was a treat as they cringed and winced under a tongue lashing.

'Take no notice of the little bleeder' the ginger fly weight's Ma told Myrtle.

'He's all mawth an' trawsers and as useless as a one legged footballer' she added demolishing a lemon sherbet, her cowed son sliding down under the sheet to hide his scarlet face.

Although Poplar was regarded as a poor inner city Borough it was blessed with a profusion of mature trees along its highways and byways. Skeletal in winter, green in spring, flowering in summer and forming golden groves in their autumn glory they became an orthopaedic nightmare as October winds stripped the branches bare and the fallen leaves became sodden and slippery. From Halloween through November the Ward saw its annual influx of the 'Leaf Skaters' or 'Suicide Shoppers' as the doddery elderly ('I only just popped aut for the paper luv') filled the beds with fractured femurs and Casualty with Colles and Smith's fractures. It was with these patients that the Physiotherapists and Nurses worked hardest, primarily to prevent hypostatic pneumonia, but also to get them mobile and back home again. Motivated by a fear of dying in a hospital that some of their age still regarded as 'The Asylum', they made very compliant patients.

To counterbalance these we had several children in traction who were more than happy to scourge us. Children in traction were a nightmare and I could now understand why the Paeds didn't want them on their Ward. The safety checks alone were onerous. At least adults understood the importance of maintaining the pull of the traction and of ensuring that they did not contort their body in any way that damaged the blood or nerve supply to limb or spine, children emulated Houdini or their super hero 'Spider Man' doing everything in their power to circumvent the objectives of putting them in traction in the first place. In a pre Play Leaders and Educational input era Bertha tolerated relaxed visiting hours, but not all parents availed of it, and I don't blame them. Why should they spend time at the bedside of a child, who, more often than not, had been up to some mischief that had put him in Sankey's in the first place? They had plenty more children at home to care for, so why not let this one torment the nurses? He'd be home and under their feet soon enough anyway. And it usually was a 'he'.

A lot more was expected of girls. From the age of 8y onwards they had household responsibilities which included caring for younger siblings. The result of these expectations usually resulted in erratic schooling and the loss of a carefree childhood but at least it kept them out of Sankey's.

The only fire drill I ever participated in was when I was on Sankey's. We came nowhere the evacuation time set but had much innocent fun for days afterwards deciding who we would, and wouldn't, save if the occasion presented itself. A raise of the eyebrows and an enquiring look from colleagues being pestered by a particular patient elicited a variety of responses

'Maybe'

'Not a chance'

'Last in line'

'Hell would freeze over first'

'What's the joke' the Orang-utan asked Myrtle?

Chapter 21

Third Years

By the spring of 1959 our Set, reduced to a baker's dozen, was several months into our third year and could see an end to our training in sight. Most of us had opted to remain living in 'Ollaway' under the watchful eyes of Bette and Joan but were cute enough to keep under their radar, if not out of trouble. Our curfew was still 10.30pm with prearranged permission to stay out until 11.00pm but I still found staying at Minty's preferable to the long journey back from Clapham, breaking the curfew, and climbing through windows. I was not alone in not seeing the witching hour as a guarantee of our chastity. There is nothing you can do after 10.30pm that you can't do an hour earlier. Apart from the Home's gloomy façade and restrictions it was a comfortable place to live. Its wide entrance and hallway opened into shabby but comfortable sitting rooms and the most important room of all, the Post Room with its alphabetical cubby holes which we checked several times a day. I noted from the preponderance of daughters of ancient Irish Kings that the O's and Mc's had by far the most space in the cubby holes. Having got used to the sounds of the tubes and early morning stock wagon we had now moved over to the Victorian part of the Residence as one of the perks of being a third year. This wing had bigger bedrooms and the much envied gas fires instead of radiators. Built in an odd Y shape this side of the home was so much quieter that I actually missed the railway noises. On cold winter evenings we would congregate in each other's rooms taking it in turns to buy butter, and purloin some sliced bread from the dining room to gorge ourselves on hot buttered toast. The Home had a communal kitchen on each landing which went unused except when our Empire students felt they would die from homesickness if they couldn't have some home cooking. It was here we learned to eat exotic food as we followed the mouth-watering smells to their source. Bette hated the smell of curry so the slightest hint would have her storming around with the window pole opening windows but Joan was not averse to a little helping of Vindaloo or Jerk Chicken so went around closing them again.

We had reasons for thinking a bit more kindly about both of them following the death of a fellow student (Mary Mac) a few sets ahead of us. About to go home on holiday she had avoided going to see Joan in the Infirmary when she felt unwell. Believing her to have departed on holiday the maid allocated to that corridor of rooms left cleaning her room to the end of her shift. By then a comatose Mary was beyond help dying from a virulent dose of meningococcal meningitis. It was an isolated case, particularly since most adults above 25y have a natural immunity to that meningococcal strain, but Mary was a bare 21y. Bette and Joan came into their own not only providing tea and sympathy but finding rooms in the Sister's Residence for Mary's family when they arrived for the post mortem and to take the body home. I remember a collection being made for her burial expenses but it was Grace Laing who found the bulk of the money needed to take Mary back to Ireland. Eileen Williamson represented the Hospital at the funeral a gesture that was typical of how seriously our welfare was considered. Galling as we found it to be answerable to Bette and Joan most of us had not yet reached the age of majority. Shortly after Mary's death a second year nurse

(Winnie) collapsed at breakfast and was found to have galloping consumption. This created a panic involving re-doing all our Mantoux tests and chest x-rays. We were all clear but we learned to value health in a personal way. Up to then we had been invincible looking after the sick without considering the consequences, now we felt we were just as likely to be a morbidity or mortality statistic.

By the third year creed lines and race lines were put aside as Sets formed their own cliques offering each other mutual practical help and asking questions of each other. In the classroom theory continued to be delivered by the nurse tutors with some sessions provided by medical doctors and other health professionals, the most memorable being Mr. Barclays post-mortems. Eileen still scrutinised our clinical practice but those who had been on the ward slightly longer than another sought each other out to ask questions rather than appear foolish in front of her or Sister, and passed on vital survival skills and the intricacies of each newly acquired clinical skill to each other. We also had a status to maintain with dozens of first and second years coming along behind us scrutinising our practice.

Like most East Enders we seldom ventured 'Up West'. Our paltry rate of remuneration meant we shopped in our local street markets with the occasional foray up to Gamages in Holborn, or 'The Co-op' in Stratford where I became the proud possessor of a book for collecting Green Shield Stamps. With the cheap schmutter on the Roman and Petticoat Lane we dressed to the nines. Having spent a childhood dreading shopping expeditions with my Gran some of her seamstress expertise and frugality had rubbed off on me and I was now a connoisseur of good cloth and finishes, and knowledgeable enough to examine the warp and the weft as well as overlocked seams and the alignment of any pattern. Alas my taste was my own so I had to learn to live with an orange mohair coat as luminous as a Belisha beacon. Setting it off was a black sequined bolero, cinched purple dirndl skirt flounced out by a cerise multi-layered net petticoat. The latter was starched with sugar to stop it drooping. This was not a good idea as I found when I had to deal with the dire consequences one humid evening when I stuck to the leatherette seat of a 25 bus.

Social life was too full for our long hours and erratic off duty but it was varied and cheap. The flighty dancers among us probably spent the most having to find the entrance price for the Gresham, Hibernian, Shamrock and Galtimore unless they got a lad from home to pay for them. However this cramped their style, and the opportunity to find a mark to buy their drinks. Although we were invited to Police and Firemen's Balls and Medical Students Hops the nurses at The London made quite sure we knew that we were encroaching on their territory in this domain. Being home-grown, middle class and on the lookout for suitable husbands they had an advantage, but we were brighter, better trained and finding husbands was not very high on our agendas. Having been given the chance of a career by Grace Laing we were not about to forgo our opportunities, well not unless one of us did something thoroughly stupid.

The West End Theatres Group was generous with free Matinée seats and tickets for previews of new shows, and local cinemas with splendid names like the Empire, Regal, Coronet, Rivoli and Troxy gave us special prices for the first showing of the day. We used the latter if we were on a split shift but being constantly tired usually slept through the programme. I remember sleeping through 'Gigi' twice in one week.

Split shifts in summer saw us flaunting our swim suits around the Lido in Victoria Park or listening to the Band Concerts there on Sunday afternoons.

My most enjoyable pastime was roller skating. I had discovered a Skating Rink in nearby Stratford so Nancy Kavanagh and I passed happy hours skating round and round with effortless grace like George and Gladys Werner. My multi-layered cerise petticoat floated and swayed on Nancy's slim body as she twirled and pirouetted through the skaters. I never wore it again after having to step out of it in full view of the other passengers on a 25 bus.

The Nurses Home itself has enough communal space to accommodate socialising. There were two sitting rooms, one for dancing to record music or watching television, the second for sitting around talking or listening to the radio. We had to be fully dressed to use either room in case anybody saw us from the small visitor's room opposite Bette's Office. Boyfriends were allowed to hover there but must never cross the boundary of the Minton tiles. Staff Nurses and Sisters had their own social space so as third years we had now reached the hierarchical eminence of having the cheek to tune the radio to Radio Luxemburg or change over the TV channel (not that we were spoiled for choice!). We used to laugh with scorn at the supposed reality of 'Emergency Ward Ten' and pick holes in the acting.

'Wodja look at the way that one is taking a blood pressure'?

'That's a rectal thermometer she's stuck in that mans gob'

'Look at the makeup on ye'r wan, ye could plaster a room with that amount of pancake'.

'She'd never get away with a uniform that short in this place'.
'Wodja take a gander at that fringe, she must be responsible for more contagion than Typhoid Mary'.
I took a look at the offending fringe and the glorious blonde bouffant hairstyle beneath a miniscule cap as a line from William Butler Yeats came to mind;
'Only God, my dear, could love you for yourself alone and not for your yellow hair'…
Ah, happy days.
And I was happier still after a sun speckled month at home in May where I had given some serious thought to future training plans and my relationship with Minty. I now knew he was not somebody I would spend a lifetime across a kitchen table from, and with the probability of him being accepted for training at the Royal College of Surgeons in Dublin our paths would naturally diverge when the Irish Sea was between us. In fact, for the next two months circumstances saw to it that we were like ships that pass in the night, he, toing and froing between London and Dublin and me sleeping my life away while I got used to on-call shifts.

Chapter 22

The Operating Theatres.

On return from holiday I found I had been allocated to the Carvery for Operating Theatre experience. I hadn't liked Theatres at St. Anne's having no idea why nurses would want to specialise in Theatre Nursing since there is little or no nursing involved. I found it technical, egotistical and elitist and suitable only for the right handed. But perhaps the She Devil Sister who had been in charge had coloured my experience so I was willing to give the new department an unbiased try.

The sheer variety of the work made theatres at St. Andrew's a lot more interesting than I anticipated and the camaraderie surprised me. With everybody wearing scrubs hierarchical uniforms and caps meant nothing, your skills took precedence and teaching was the remit of the Sister in charge of a particular speciality. There was going to be no Eileen Williamson to keep us up to scratch here. We went from washing walls to packing drums, autoclaving to counting instruments, setting trolleys to gowning up, dirty nurse to clean nurse, and the most nerve racking of all, the Tally Nurses assistant. The shift in the balance of power moved from the surgeon to Tally Nurse as she accounted for swabs and instruments at the end of an operation. No patient could be sewn up until she announced 'Tally complete'. It took some guts to keep a God waiting but the philosophy was 'Black looks couldn't kill but a Spenser Wells in the gut could'.

St. Andrews Theatres did have one thing in common with St. Anne's and that was the end of operating session routine. The mantra was the same;

If you can see it clean it
If you can't see it clean it

If you can reach it clean it
If you can't reach it clean it
If it's made of stainless steel scrub it
If it is made from rubber, soak it
If it is used replace it
If it is not used recycle it

One of the advantages of training in a District Hospital was that, unlike our fellow nursing students at The London, which was a teaching hospital, we were not vying with dozens of medical students for experience. Yes, we had our quota, but we also had the advantage of Grace Laing encouraging the Ward Sisters to free up time to allow us to go to post mortems or Consultants teaching sessions, and so it was in Theatres. Notwithstanding all the hard work we had plenty of opportunity to observe the surgeons at work and note their idiosyncrasies, eccentricities and egos. They all had their favourite instruments and trolley lay out, not to mention their favourite scrub nurse who could of course read their mind no matter how often they changed it. One Consultant preferred to dispense with scrub trousers preferring to wear boxer shorts under his gown to 'keep a cool head'. In the heat of summer with the sun beating down on our outsize windows I envied him the choice. As for egos, God's Gift was as temperamental as a movie star throwing instruments over his shoulder if sister had the temerity to anticipate his needs. I was busy replenishing her tray when he roared for a retractor. She looked to me to scuttle off and get one.

'Where is the retractor' he bellowed glaring at me as I turned to go?

Hot, bothered and enraged and throwing caution to the wind I shouted back

'It's on the feckin floor behind you'.

You could have heard a pin drop as he looked at me over his half moon specs.
There was a united exhalation of breath as he laughed and said humourously 'So it is Nurse, so it is.'
I began to understand why he was dubbed 'God's Gift'
Apart from these moments of diversion we learned to be bored to death by the surgeons golfing, sailing and rugby narrations, however face masks cover a multitude of expressions but as long as you could keep a spark of interest in your eyes you were fairly safe unless they threw an unexpected question at you. In my case it was the Thoracic surgeon who having been drivelling on about Wagner's Ring Cycle suddenly asked me to identify the symptoms of cancer of the bronchus.
'Anorexia, breathlessness, chest pain, cough, fatigue, fever and wheezing came to mind but they were all symptoms of a host of chest and lung diseases so I knew I would score no points as the words left my mouth. I was saved from ridicule by the vision of One-Step Moran, a previous patient, and his incessant hiccupping and added 'irritation of the vagus nerve' to my list of symptoms. I hoped he was not going to make a habit of quizzing me because I rather liked Thoracic surgery despite its rib cracking techniques and didn't want to limit my choices of surgery any further.
I already had a strong distaste for Orthopaedic sessions with the noise of the drills and chisels boring holes in my brain as well as the patient, and Ophthalmology made me physically ill. Eyes were done under local anaesthetic. The patients face was covered so that just the eye, clamped apart with a special retractor, was on view. Mr. Green, our Ophthalmic Consultant was a well nourished man with very big hands who sat on an adjustable stool by the patients head to operate. To watch him manipulating small delicate instruments in his sausage like fingers when removing cataracts made my stomach flip. My job was to hold the patients

hand, make light reassuring conversation and ensure the theatre light was in a prime position. Despite trying to keep my grasp relaxed and my tone of voice reassuring I knew I had failed when a patient told me that the last time a woman had held his hand like that had been his wife when she was in labour and that he still had the nail marks to prove it. I felt bad about avoiding Mr. Green's sessions. He was by far the nicest surgeon there and his expertise in his field was renowned.

By mid July I had progressed to scrubbing up for minor operations and so far had been disaster free. That was about to change. The weather was hot and the air conditioning erratic from freezing in theatres to baking in the recovery areas and instrument rooms. As well as working an eight hour shift we took it in turn to be 'on-call' for a week at a time. This could involve an hour or two for a simple appendix to four or five hours for perforated oesophageal varices or other dire emergency. Whatever the hours you were back on duty at 8.00am for a full shift and that continued until another team went on-call. At that point you got your on-call time back. This routine played havoc with our body clocks and I felt constantly tired and nauseated. After a particularly long operation I fainted, having the good sense not to contaminate anything or anybody as I slid gracefully to the floor.

I was immediately shipped off to Joan in the Infirmary where I slept around the clock to be woken only to have copious amounts of lukewarm Lukozade foisted on me. I've hated it ever since. Examined by the Resident Medical Officer I was diagnosed with anaemia and discharged with a prescription of Iron tablets and Folic Acid and found myself back on another week of 'on-call'.

With so little staff on for out-of hour's surgery there was more opportunity for us students to gain experience assisting at operations. I was promised the next appendectomy and much to my delight I would be scrubbing for my favourite Senior Houseman. My delight was not because I fancied him but because he was left handed so would not constantly turn instruments and suturing forceps around as right handed surgeons did if I inadvertently clamped them for left handed practitioners.

'Reds, when I'm a famous Consultant I'm going to employ you as my own special theatre nurse' he used to joke. However all joking ceased the night that an eleven year old lad lay in the anaesthetic room awaiting the removal of his appendix. I was so preoccupied setting out my tray of instruments that the Sister and Staff Nurse on the on-call team had the premeded boy on the table with the anaesthetist checking the readings on his Boyles machine before I noticed anything. A popular young anaesthetist he was normally full of chat but that night he seemed totally engrossed with the dials on his machine as the boy drifted into unconsciousness. The boy's abdomen was swabbed and towelled and ready for surgery.

'Ok, ready when you're ready' the Houseman said to the 'gas passer' as we facetiously referred to anaesthetists.

'Okey dokey' he responded as he tied his mask up. With this utterance a waft of alcohol came across the operation table strong enough to permeate my mask. He had drink taken. I should say that in the ethos of the time it was common for on-call doctors to drop into the local hostelry for a swift half.

But was he drunk, was he capable of doing his job, were we going to put this child's life at risk?

There was an elephant in the room and everybody was ignoring it. When I saw the Houseman reaching forward to make the incision I spoke up

'I won't take part in this operation' I said in a voice I didn't recognise.

'I don't know whether or not that child is safe in his hands' I said looking at the anaesthetist.

The anaesthetist first tried to jolly me along then tried to make me feel seriously guilty about delaying surgery on a child already under anaesthetic.

'Phone your Registrar' I advised the Houseman guessing he was out of his depth.

I looked at the Sister and Staff Nurse for guidance. I looked in vein.

'You can go back to bed Nurse' Sister told me.

As I left the changing room to return to the Nurses Home I saw her preparing to scrub up. For several days I expected to be asked to make a statement but no mention was made of the incident. The operation had gone ahead and the child had made an uneventful recovery. Life went on as before.

Should I let it go?

I remembered Sr. Josephine and the incident of a Houseman putting patients in danger of cross infection. In that instance, and in my arrogance, I felt I had had dealt with the situation by confronting him with his poor practice.

'So you took it upon yourself to decide that he had become a competent and safe practitioner', Sr. Josephine had asked me witheringly when she found out?

I knew that *anything* I said would dig my grave deeper. Why hadn't I told her?

'You also took it upon yourself to put *my* patients in jeopardy by not reporting incidents of possible cross contamination' she added?

Wasn't I doing the same thing here? Had the child been put at risk?

I was sick with worry about the possible repercussions so eventually took the problem to Eileen Williamson. Her response was factual and to the point. Apart from asking me to clarify some events she left me to write a report on what had taken place and asked me not to discuss the matter with anybody. I knew that this incident was likely to go further, but the relief of sharing my concerns was enormous. The following morning she informed me that my time in Theatres had come to an end and that I was to be sent back to the Chroni Bronies.

Later in the day Grace Laing sat me by her desk and went through my statement with me. She made no comment on my actions apart from reminding me that I should have gone to Night Sister instead of heading for bed. Night Sister would have contacted her, and the situation could have been immediately assessed. Being totally ignorant of the hierarchy between Theatre Sisters and Night Sisters I had not given it a thought or considered the possibility of Grace getting out of bed. I tried to suppress a vision of her arriving in a pink satin dressing gown to determine the drunken capabilities of the on-call anaesthetist.

I heard no more about the incident. I assume that the greater good prevailed. I also assumed that theatre would be having Matron's rounds at unexpected times.

Chapter 23

The Hollow Man

'You have a fundal height three fingers above the symphysis pubis which gestationally makes you about 16 weeks' Ernie Cooke, a local GP told me as he removed the three fingers he had been prodding into my stomach just below the umbilicus. For those of you ignorant of such matters the 'fundal height' is a measurement of the size of the uterus used to assess foetal growth and development during pregnancy. It is measured in centimetres from the top of the uterus to the top of the mother's pubic bone in line with the umbilicus.

He may as well have punched me in the solar plexus as the jolt of what he said took my breath away. I had no idea I was pregnant and had come to see him because I was still feeling continually nauseous and tired, and was losing weight. On top of this the Iron pills and Folic Acid seemed to be doing nothing apart from making me constipated. I actually feared I might have cancer so I suppose pregnancy should have been a relief.

But it wasn't.

As I got re-dressed to say that my reaction was one of disbelief, devastation and shock was the understatement of the century. Beyond not being married, I wasn't ready for a child. I was about to embark on a career which did not include husbands or babies for the foreseeable future. From this day forward I would no longer have the luxury of that independence or freedom of choice. I thought of all the things I had planned which would now be pie in the sky. I was going to be trapped into motherhood. Racking my brain trying to fathom how I had conceived I went over and over the facts and came to the conclusion it could only have occurred in the week before ovulation at the end of April, or in other words, the good old catholic safe period because, unless it was an Immaculate Conception, I was in my own chaste childhood bed in Dublin for the following month. Any woman with a regular menstrual cycle is usually liable to get pregnant about 5 days each month, when ovulation occurs. On average, ovulation occurs midway through the menstrual cycle. Because sperm can live for 3 to 5 days in a woman's reproductive tract, it is possible to become pregnant if intercourse occurs several days before ovulation. In this instance the sperm must have been virile enough to survive 7days. Only somebody as cursed as me could get pregnant in *that* time frame.

'Did you not consider that you might be pregnant' he asked me?

I suppose in my heart of hearts I had, but I associated pregnancy with morning sickness and amenorrhea and while I had been continually vomiting throughout the day, mornings were my best times. I was also having light menstrual bleeding which the Resident Medical Office had put down to anaemia. I now learned I had been suffering from 'hyperemesis gravidarum', dehydration and 'spotting' from a low placenta'. Some nurse I was, some diagnostician the RMO!

The previous week Minty had heard that he had been accepted by Royal College of Surgeons Medical School so a farewell party was planned at the India Club the coming Friday. Not wanting to break the news in front of others I arranged to meet for tea at Lyon's Corner House. I had never seen him so happy and animated. We had already made plans to keep in touch when he had told me about his success and prospective move to Dublin. I had been genuinely pleased for him and although nothing was said I think we had come to the conclusion that no serious relationship would continue between us but that we would remain good friends.

I will never forget the look of shock on his face as I told him I was pregnant. I thought he was going to have a heart attack.

'What are you going to do' he asked? Noting the singular I blamed myself for the use of the words 'I'm pregnant' instead of 'we're going to become parents'.
'I'm going ahead with the pregnancy' I told him.
'You don't have to' he said quietly 'I'll find the money'.
Having spent three months on the Gynae Ward dealing with the horrors of back street abortionists I was stunned to think he would even consider the possibility, but I suppose it was the only way he saw of confronting the situation. I believe he could see his world crumbling if I pursued him for support, or brought the matter to the attention of the Dean at the Royal College who would throw him out on his ear. His brain seemed drunk with panic as he made hard work of lifting a cup to his lips.
'I've got to go' he told me making to leave
'We'll talk later'.
As I finished my tea, trying to stem an urge to cry, I knew we would never have that talk.

For the next three months I totally ignored the fact that I was pregnant. I was back on night duty floating between 'K' and 'L' surgical wards. Apart from having to expand the length of my grosgrain belt and wear a roll-on I had no difficulty hiding my rising bump. However with two weeks of final block and hospital finals coming up I knew there was no way I was going to escape Eileen Williamson's beady eye during a fortnight in the classroom. But the catalyst for action was when I was lying in the bath watching my stomach move as my seven month baby stretched in bliss released from the confines of the cage of my well developed abdominal muscles. I decided that I had to face up to the reality of my pregnancy so I did as many a girl in my situation did. I wrote to Evelyn Home, the Agony Aunt in 'Woman' magazine asking for help. This brought back memories of a more innocent time when my cousin Bridgie and I used to read Evelyn's problem page across Aunt Sarah's table tutting at stupid girls who had 'eaten of the forbidden fruit' and were now no better than harlots. By return of post, in a plain brown envelope was a personal reply from Evelyn inviting me to contact her and advising that I tell somebody I could trust as soon as possible. She had included in the envelope a referral for me to give to the hospital Lady Almoner explaining the current circumstances. Setting the ball rolling was only a start. I still had to face Eileen Williamson and eventually Grace Laing.

As if I didn't have enough to contend with I had another run in with Blondie. Relieving on night duty on her Ward I noticed the light on in her office and opened the door to turn it off. Unfortunately I opened it some seconds too soon. She had her back to me busy removing food from a shelf in store cupboard. Several items were already on her desk next to a large shopping bag. I saw momentary panic in her eyes before she went on the offensive asking me what I wanted. As I watched she calmly put the packages back on the shelf. I could prove nothing but I knew, and she knew she I knew. Grace Laing wasn't the only one who could act for the greater good.

Limehouse Lil was not noted for her liking for Blondie but she was a conscientious Ward Maid as protective of her patient's welfare as a lioness was of her cubs so having to creep and crawl to get enough tea or jam from Blondie galled her. Letting her know what I had witnessed gave me the greatest pleasure. I knew that she would make good use of the information. As my Granda used to say 'There's more than one way to skin a cat'.

Revenge is a dish best served as humble pie so I knew Lil would do me proud.

Chapter 24

Moral Welfare

The East end of London had been the focus of 'do gooders' for more than a century so were well used to the checks and barriers they endured to ensure they, the recipients, were worthy of this largesse. The philanthropic profession of Lady Almoners appealed to women who were interested in pursuing a career in social work because it offered opportunities to ameliorate social evils and benefit the worthy poor at the same time. In 1907 the establishment of a Hospital Almoners' Council for the training of candidates gave a great impetus to their employment within the hospital setting. It was a post with considerable power because the post holder was only answerable to the Charity Organisation Commission, an offshoot of the Poor Law Commissioners whereas Matron, for all her power, was answerable to the Hospital Board.

Pre National Health Service the Hospital Almoner has a two-fold duty to perform; she has to protect the interests of the hospital by eliminating unsuitable cases seeking free treatment, ensuring that those who could afford it contributed toward the expenses of their treatment.

She is probably better remembered in her post NHS work on behalf of the patients themselves. All applications for admission into convalescent homes passed through her hands, and in suitable cases she made grants from the Samaritan Fund, patients being required to contribute, if possible, according to their means. She would be particularly recalled by consumptives and rickety children. The hospital doctor having perhaps, prescribed a diet of rich in eggs and milk he might just as well ordered champagne and caviar, the patient being as little able to afford one as the other, so if extra nourishment was required as part of the treatment, she provided a voucher for its purchase. To be seen queuing outside her Office in Outpatients labelled you as a 'Charity Case' but to be taken on by her service swallowing ones pride was the price you paid. She also provided for home nursing where necessary or called on the assistance of the health visitor and sometimes even temporary domestic help. She was expected to be a mine of information on charitable organisations, friendly societies and to have influence in the Labour Exchange. A man in the hospital for weeks could well lose his employment so to send him out without any prospect of work often meant his speedy return and that in a worse state than before. In such a case the Almoner provided a chitty for one of the labour exchanges, and work was often found for him as soon as he was discharged.

Her closest association was probably with the Moral Welfare Association who were then working from an office in the Roman Road. Moral Welfare Workers, the Church of England equivalent of a social worker, were allocated to the Maternity Unit and Gynaecology Ward using a section of the Almoners Department as well as their Office on 'the Roman' to see their clients. I can't remember what was etched on their frosted window but to be seen going into their Office was as stigmatising as entering a Lombard's with its pawnbrokers' three sphere symbol suspended from a bar for all to see because they also worked in venereal disease hospitals befriending and providing after-care for women.

In addition the MWA had a role dealing with women who got pregnant out of wedlock. I was soon to discover this first hand when I glided discretely through their Roman Road door. Depending on your point of view, they were either guardian angels or truancy officers. Their hierarchy, the Diocesan Moral Education Committees were Church of England led and funded. The Second World War had brought an increase in the number of illegitimate children and this led to a change in the focus of their work. Where previously the mother's right to keep the child and the father's duty to maintain it were pursued, more thought was now given to the welfare and future of the baby, which meant that where appropriate adoption was encouraged.

In 1943 the Ministry of Health had placed statutory obligations on Local Authorities to provide welfare services for unmarried mothers and children so the Diocesan Committee were paid regular grants by the London County Council to provide the service. Like the Health Care system of the time and its many training routes into nursing there was nearly as many specialisms in Social Services. There was no such thing as a Generic Social Worker. That didn't come about until 1975.

I can't remember the chronology of activating Evelyn Home's suggestion but I told Eileen Williamson first. Not a flicker of surprise or condemnation crossed her face as she looked me up and down

'About 32 weeks I'd say' she surmised.

Spot on.

She got up to lock her office door so that we wouldn't be disturbed and I told her of events to date. When I got to my reliance on the safe period her response was apt

'Using the safe period is as reliable as telling the time from a dandelion clock' she pontificated scathingly.

Establishing the fact that my baby was not for adoption she persuaded me that the first thing I must establish was what help I could expect from my extended family. In the meantime I should continue my training as long as possible to have a hope of qualifying.

Several long days passed before replies from the family filtered back. They varied from

'Let us rear the child for you'.

'Have the baby adopted and make a fresh start'
'Come back home and say you've been widowed' to
'If you come home with a bastard I'll make sure you end up in a Magdalene Convent'.
I suppose those responses represented a good cross section of society at the time and clarified my options.

When I was summoned to Grace Laing's Office I found the Lady Almoner and Eileen Williamson already seated and observing the empty coffee cups I knew that a pre-meeting had already taken place. I remember little or nothing of the ensuing discussion but most of it was a rehash of what I had told Eileen. What I do recall was my relief that I was not being judged. The outcome was the Lady Almoner urged caution about making any decisions before the birth, Grace told me she would find a way for me to continue nursing as long as possible ensuring that any gap in training would be kept to a minimum, and that Eileen would continue to supervise me to complete the General Nursing Council curriculum requirements. I was to realise later that while both of them observed the spirit of the law, fulfilling the letter might not have stood up to detailed scrutiny by the GNC.
The next step was for the Lady Almoner to refer me to the Moral Welfare Service to book a place in a Mother and Baby Home, and for me to get through a fortnight in the School of Nursing and Hospital Finals.

My Moral Welfare Worker, Margaret, was a cheerful, buxom young woman with a holiness proclaiming her as 'Gods Elect' written all over her zealously scrubbed face. She was humanised by a liking for cats and Liquorish Allsorts. However all I wanted from her was that she showed understanding and was knowledgeable, efficient and proficient. She was all of those and more as she guided me through the bureaucracy of Maternity

Benefit, choice of Mother and Baby Home and the Fostering Service.

Grace was as good as her word and arranged a transfer to Glebe House a Convalescent Home out in the sticks. With six week to term I would live in and work there for as long as possible and attend a local Maternity Unit for ante-natal care before entering a Mother and Baby Home. The Ante-Natal Clinic was the only place I was 'branded' when the Clinic Sister deliberately called out 'Miss Redmond' across the waiting room.

'She's a UM' she told the Consultant, and I knew she didn't mean Unaccompanied Minor. The only thing of interest to her was my stomach which she examined with unusual roughness. The only thing of interest to me was booking a bed for delivery because I had no intention of ever returning to the Clinic fearing if I did so that I would scratch her scornful eyes out.

Chapter 25

Mother and Baby

The 'Arrow-on-de-'Ill Mother and Baby Home was affiliated to the Harrow-on-the-Hill Anglican Church and run by a Matron who oversaw its Christian principals and led the daily prayer meeting. By the standards of the day, it was a benign regime but with many infertile couples desperate to adopt, like other Homes, they favoured adoption so inmates would find themselves pressed to give up their child.

Having said that, it was against the Homes policy to accept a fee from adoptive parents - thus removing the motive many homes had to encourage women to give up their child. Each mother was allowed six weeks after the birth to decide what to do, however, fear of being judged by society meant that most never felt free to explore their options, even tho' they were they informed of their rights, entitlements and any alternatives to adoption.

When I was admitted to the Home with two weeks to go to term, the ante-natal bed spaces were already filled with girls well established in the daily routine. It was usual for girls to take up a place as soon as their Maternity Benefit started which was at 34 weeks gestation. Board and Lodging was deducted from this weekly Benefit if you had employment stamps, for those too young to have worked it came out of the 'National Welfare System'.

Known to its neighbours as the 'Unmarried Mothers Home' the big sprawling detached house on Roxborough Park was home to 27 or so girls ranging in age from 17 to 42 years. Although there were no physical obstructions within the Home to keep ante-natal's and post-natal's separated they saw little of each other apart from eating together and sharing a sitting room. It wasn't until I had given birth that I realised that post-natally we were very different people and I'm ashamed to say we had no patience with those awaiting the rite of passage when we only had six weeks to make life altering decisions.

With some this decision was a foregone conclusion. Their desire to keep the shame of a pregnancy a secret overrode all other considerations; their baby's would be adopted.

The youngest were coerced into secrecy by their parents and were blackmailed on all sides into giving their baby up by providing it with 'the best chance in life'. The rest of us were a mixed bag of the hopeful and determined; some would succeed, some would bow beneath the pressure of society and battles with the Labour and Welfare System.

State support was so meagre that most single mothers could only realistically afford to keep their babies if the extended family came to the rescue. The ethos of the time was to prioritise the deserving poor so immigrants and unwed mothers got scant regard. There was at least free Day Nursery provision but that was of little use if you couldn't find housing, or jobs with hours to suit, and since the Nurseries closed at the slightest hint of contagion job security was constantly put at risk by these erratic closures.

Fostering was an expensive and worrying option being mostly unregulated and unsupervised. Constantly worrying about your baby's welfare was another reason why girls took the adoption route even though it broke their heart and led to a lifetime of guilt and regret.

They could of course have sued the father for support but this had to be in open court and could be reported in the local paper bringing shame on the family.

If it hadn't been for Eileen Williamson's advice I could have ended up in a more oppressive Catholic Crusade of Rescue Home run by Nuns where I would have been treated as a "fallen woman" and would have little choice but to hand my baby over to a couple in exchange for a handsome "donation" to the organization whose main function was to protect the faith of children born to mothers mired in sin. To ensure this the majority of the children were sent to Ireland or further afield to languish in Institutions until a good Catholic home was found. My own family adopted five such children.

As I heard my baby's first cry my heart overflowed with love as the midwife placed the precious bundle in my arms. Nothing else was as important as her welfare. Although I had six weeks to make plans I would not have the luxury of that amount of time away from training if I wanted to complete the SRN course. I did not even consider adoption so it would have to be short term fostering or sending her home until I could see past my need to qualify.

I had a letter from Grace Laing congratulating me on a safe confinement and asking me to come to see her. It was at this meeting that I realised that even if I managed to complete my training there was no future for me in nursing. The hours alone would see to that. If I was to raise a child it would have to involve long term foster care or separation. She advocated sending my baby home, sharing with me the fact that her grandmother, finding herself in a similar situation had sent the baby, her father, back to Scotland to be raised within the family. I knew that I did not have the strength of will to do this. I also knew that were I to move back to Dublin I would be a burden on my Grandmother until I found work. Beginning to despair I was tempted to take up the offer of a much loved cousin to rear my baby down the bogs of Galway. I knew this would be an ideal solution but was too selfish to contemplate it.

While all this was going on I was being gently persuaded by my Moral Welfare Worker to 'consider the baby's best interests and

opportunities' and be less absorbed in my own selfish wishes. She's very lucky I didn't deck her.
It was Eileen Williamson as usual who came to the rescue. Phoning me at the Home she told me in her fast Cork accent to
'Git hawld ofde Avenin Sthandarth and raid de Houshkeepers wanted shection deres ajob rite up ye'r sthraight'.
Deciphering this as
'Get hold of an Evening Standard and read the 'Housekeepers Wanted' section. There is a job right up your street.
And so there was. 'Mothers Help is required by professional family with five children in West Dulwich. Applicant will be expected to live en famille. Own child welcome. Apply in writing to Box 3531. Closing date 28-02-1960
The job was mine.

Chapter 26

EPILOGUE

The day I closed the door to a career in nursing I opened the door to an unknown future. I took a deep breath and stepped through it to start a new life. The world turns as it must so it would be 13 years before I had the opportunity of returning to complete my training. In that period many changes had taken place in the NHS. Advances in surgical techniques on the heart and lungs had become commonplace and led to the opening of coronary care wards and thoracic surgical units. Intensive care specialism progressed in tandem with neurosurgery and traumatic orthopaedic surgery. Genitourinary and paediatric surgery were also becoming the province of specialist rather than general surgeons as individual doctors pushed themselves and their expertise out of enlightened self-interest. The Juju men now had the advantage of pharmacology supporting advancements in technology with the division of general pathology into biochemistry, histopathology, haematology and microbiology.

Grace Laing retired before her time due to ill health and Eileen Williamson followed her perhaps seeing the writing on the wall when the Matron who replaced Grace lost the goodwill of the staff by making it known that there would be no more recruiting abroad. By 1963, St. Andrews, administered by the No 8 Group, Bow Hospital Management Committee was no longer able to provide the range of experience required for State Registration so lost its mandate from the GNC to train student nurses. Then, following the recommendations of the 1964 Platt Report it was granted the status of a pupil nurse training hospital to train Enrolled Nurses. Two years on, the Salmon Report of 1966 recommended a change to the senior nursing structure which effectively heralded the end of the traditional matron role. With no central person in charge of the standard of nursing care it devolved to administrators consumed by bureaucracy who didn't necessarily have nursing or hospital experience. It's truly shameful how much pointless upheaval and change has taken place in the NHS. To this day people are bemoaning the loss of Matrons and bedside nursing but rest assured, Reader, as you lie dying from neglect on a hospital ward your 'named' nurse whom you may never actually see, will have a university degree! You may never hear the word 'patient' or 'care' used because you have become a 'consumer of a set of targets.

St Andrews became the Hospital nobody wanted. Although geographically in Poplar the 1974 NHS reorganisation 'gave' the hospital to Newham Health District under the City and East London Area Health Authority (Teaching) reshuffle. Then in 1974 this Group merged with the West Ham Group to form the Thames Group of Hospitals and following a further realignment in 1982 it was bequeathed to Newham Health Authority to administer. They made use of the old School of Nursing by transferring the headquarters of the Newham District School of Nursing to the site in 1985. Here, at my old Alma Mater, I found myself lecturing to a group of students with the same skeletal gentleman in the corner, looking none the worse for wear, so obviously still free from desecration. I could feel the sardonic presence of Eileen Williamson beside him and hoped that she would think I had done well. The expansion of the A12 Blackwall Tunnel approach road from a two lane road to a six lane highway at its back entrance made access to St. Andrews difficult and allowed it to slip in to decay, demise and dereliction, finally being abandoned in 2006. Condemned due to its age and state of disrepair it was razed to the ground in 2009.

I was very fortunate to have trained at St. Andrews. In 1950's there was not many hospital Matrons or teachers who would show such compassion and understanding to a student in my circumstances. It would have been instant dismissal, no reference and banishment to whence they came.

I learned that raising a child was hard work but that you adapt and stop thinking it is the end of the world. You accept that the path you have taken is not the one you intended to take embark on but that the journey is what you make it. I eventually got where I wanted by a very circuitous route and I wouldn't have had it any other way.

Notes

Liquor sauce is made from the left over water that the eels were cooked in, thickened with corn flour it has a handful of chopped parsley added which gives it its vibrant green hue. Whatever goodness the parsley might add is more than countermanded by its high salt content, and bicarbonate, added to maintain its colour while destroying its Vit C content.

Thrown on Life's 'Surge 'Custody of the Eyes'. For those of you who do not know or have long since forgotten, to practise Custody of the Eyes is the duty of a religious, not only because it is necessary for their own improvement in virtue, but also because it is an example for the edification of others.

I Dreamt I Dwelt in Marble Halls (a memoir of a Dublin childhood) I always took note of Annie Walker's sagacious reminder to me to carry 'mad' money. 'Don't be dependent on any louser seeing you home; always stick your fare home in your bra if you're going on a date'.

1-2 weeks blocks of teaching were interspersed between our ward allocations. The PTS being constantly in use our Blocks were held in an empty 3rd floor ward which we shared with racks of artificial limbs and shelves of orthopaedic shoes.

The Summer Children (a memory of my grandmother's funeral in Claregalway) 'Her coffin was raised up on the jaunting car and strapped on. The pony set off for the Church, and we all prepared to follow, however with the first turn of the wheels the coffin started to slide, and despite being adjusted it continued to lurch from side to side, every step foretelling disaster. I don't know which of us started laughing first, but Tommy Duggan and I were soon consumed by rippling waves of hysteria that kept surging up past our vocal cords until we were whooping and bent over with mirth. In the midst of this madness I saw we were being observed, and given 'The Basilisk Glare' by our respective mother's. Our laughter was infectious and some of the onlookers began to smile and enjoy a bit of craic. Peggy, the collie, began to dance around and bark with excitement. Nothing short of a good slapping or a bucket of cold water over our heads was going to stop Tommy and me. It was I who got my legs skelped *and* a bite from a manic Peggy for good measure'.

The Hollow Man 'Ever note, Lucilius, 'When love begins to sicken and decay it useth an enforced ceremony. There are no tricks in plain and simple faith, but hollow men, like horses hot at hand make gallant show and promise of their mettle; but when they should endure the bloody spur, they fall their crests, and like deceitful jades sink in the trial."

Source: William Shakespeare; Julius Caesar (Brutus at IV, ii)

A PROMISE OF TOMORROWS

Chapter 1

Wildlife in SE21

Two pair of eyes stared unblinkingly at me seated on one of the back side seats of a battered twelve seater yellow Bedford van. They knelt facing me on the middle seat to scrutinize me in comfort. My month old daughter slept in her bassinette beside me while on the opposite seat a carrycot held an eight month baby, arms above his head and dead to the world apart from the occasional gentle sucking movements he made with his mouth.

'Sit down' the driver said firmly to the kneeling children, who totally ignored her.

'I only brought three of them in case you changed your mind if you met them en masse' she said cheerfully looking back at me through the van mirror.

My new employer, Ann, was a well built, bohemian looking woman, with hair twisted into an untidy bun, a face free of any trace of makeup and full of character rather than beauty. A doctor, with five children under ten, she handled the cumbersome van expertly and without apparent effort on our journey from Harrow-on-the-Hill to West Dulwich.

I had previously been to the Dulwich house to be interviewed so knew what to expect. On that occasion the three older children had been in Sussex with their grandmother and the younger ones sleeping. Shabby and untidy the house had seemed quiet and peaceful. My daughter and I would be expected to live en famille with me employed as 'mothers help'. My room on the second floor was spacious and warm and overlooked the road and obliquely, Dulwich College Prep School. I would share this landing with Jane age four and, John, the baby who was currently sleeping in the dressing room adjacent to his parent's bedroom would join us as soon as I had settled in. There was bathroom across the landing, a single bedroom converted into a kitchen and two double bedrooms, one housing Jane.

Peter, father of the children, had been inveigled out of his study near the end of the interview to give me the once over. A thin dark haired man in a leg iron, and also a doctor, he scrutinized me as thoroughly as his children were now doing.

'Your application makes you sound as if you can do everything apart from walk on water' he said humorously.

'Well, given time I'll probably master that too' I responded smartly much to his amusement.

His easy charm and droll sense of humour immediately put me at ease but disconcerted Ann because he began regaling me with horror stories about previous employees who had fled unable to cope with their children's unruly behaviour, and the lack of routine and consistently in the household.

A small grimy hand held out a match box towards me and said invitingly

'Would you like to see inside?'

I saw the glint of devilment in the eyes of the grubby handed blonde eight year old and remembered my Cousin Tommy Duggan's frog collection.

'Ok, let's have a look' I said encouragingly.

With his thumb he gently pushed the matchbox open while holding it out in my direction. Much to his disappointment the ensuing screams were not from me but from the four year old Jane who took a flying leap into one of the front passenger seats of the van causing her mother to veer wildly across the road and yell impotently at her. Mid Sunday afternoon the traffic was sparse which probably saved our lives because seat belts were non mandatory in 1960.

‘Wow, he’s a monster’ I said nonchalantly reaching over and touching the pincer of an enormous shiny stag beetle which filled the box.

‘Isn’t he a bit uncomfortable in there’ I asked without engaging my brain.

‘Probably’ said the budding entomologist as he tipped him out on my hand.

I knew this was a make or break moment and watched the look of glee turn to disappointment as I failed to react.

‘It would be kinder to let him go’ I told the little provoker as I offered the beetle back to him.

Thus was my first encounter with Mark’s wild life enthusiasm. It was to be the first of many.

Other books by author

I Dreamt I Dwelt in Marble Halls

The rent of 3s.6d a week in the Dublin Artisans' Dwelling Company flats was relatively high in the early 1920's when the author's grandparents moved in. Built to house artisans the tenancies were beyond the means of labourer's who earned about a £1 a week.

On the death of her mother in 1947 she moved from nearby Upper Rutland St. to live in the Dwellings with her grandparents and remembers it as a matriarchal enclave where the women castigated and cursed each other's children and minded them when necessary. They criticized one another, supported one another through the 'nagers', delivered babies when a 'Bona Fide' midwife wasn't available or couldn't be afforded, borrowed and lent finery, often taken out of the Pawn for the occasion, and laid out and waked the dead. The Memoir is rich in humour and historical lore for those who remember Summerhill, the Dwellings, the nearby Streets, the Tin Church, and the choice of schools like the Red Brick Slaughter House, the Sado Brothers or the love 'em or hate 'em Nuns in North William Street. It will lead you down a path of nostalgia you cannot fail to enjoy. For others it's a series of glimpses of North Dublin communal life that for once does not include vermin, abuse, neglect or a granny who was a dealer. It also encompasses vignettes of family members bringing them to life to be remembered fondly with wry recognition of their faults and foibles. We are introduced to characters like Annie Lawlor, Nick Colgan and the Grant and Breslin families and will meet some of them again in 'Thrown on Life's Surge'.

The Summer Children

This book is a memoir of long summer holidays the author spent in Claregalway with her mother's family from 1944 to the mid 1950's. Living in an inner city area in Dublin this annual holiday was like another world where she, and her two siblings, ran free and wild ignoring edicts to keep away from the river, stay out of field with the bull in it, not to eat or drink anything from Bina Lenihan's kitchen and not to annoy the neighbours. Lying about these activities was enough to ensure that she, and her co-conspirators, had sufficient sins to make a weekly confession worthwhile.

As self-centered children they were not aware of the struggles and sacrifices of their hardworking family who farmed the land and slaned the turf in the townlands of Gortcloonmore, Gortadooey, Montiagh, Cregboy and Cloonbiggen, the latter in the townland of Claregalway, all, within the Parish of Claregalway.

Today the old Claregalway townlands are little more than names on a map vying for space with new housing estates, and a simple way of life has long gone. Local characters are remembered by fewer and fewer people but for those who do remember them they are recalled with great affection.

In an era when people stopped for the angelus bell and when money only changed hands on Fair and Quarter Days neighbour harvested with neighbour, divided butchered meat and Hughes Shop put weekly necessities 'on the ledger' until customers had the where-with-all to settle the account. ***Living as we do now in money and possession driven times a look back on a simpler life is a salutary experience. As her***

Dublin Gran was wont to say 'You don't know where you're going unless you know where you've been' so as this memoir unravels the tricks of memory and fable, it records both sad and happy times. There is mischief aplenty, music galore, waking the dead, tales of Canon Moran and family skeletons.

Thrown on Life's Surge

This memoir is part of an Irish trilogy based on the experience and recollections of the author, a Dublin girl from Summerhill, a decaying north inner city area a short walk from the City Centre. Her first volume provides a glimpse of a Dublin childhood and family life in the Artisans Dwellings, Upper Buckingham Street in 1940's -1950's Dublin, and the second, in complete contrast, an account of running wild in the boglands of Galway during the long summer holidays. This volume covers the period of a nurse training course at St. Anne's Skin and Cancer Hospital. There, age 17y, she learned to deal with the terminally ill on a daily basis in a setting that provided dignity, comfort, camaraderie and, more surprisingly, fun.

The Nuns, her fellow probationers and the patients are all portrayed as people well remembered. The Nuns range from the 'She Devil' to the saintly and the probationers as culchie's to the core, united in their urge to escape bondage on the family farm. Stories of the patients are poignant, in particular those of Mikeen and Maggo. In contrast the humour of the deaths of Mrs. Von and the Widow Maker, and the hilarity of a Day at the Races is life affirming and funny.

A Promise of Tomorrows

As the author moves on with her dreams of a career in nursing on hold the scene shifts from London's East End across the river to the leafy suburbs of south-east London then onwards and upwards to the Mecca of the medical profession in the golden triangle that was Harley St, Wimpole St and Devonshire Place.

Working as a nanny cum housekeeper for two ambitious doctors and living en famille she takes on the responsibility of their six anarchic, unruly, bickering, lovable children.

She charts their family life through the ups and downs of thirteen eventful years with humour and perspicuity as the children protest her authority and find ingenious ways of circumventing her boundaries. Disappearing, as they were wont to do at the first sign of battle, one is left to wonder wryly why their parents had six children in the first place, since their parenting seemed peripheral to their busy professional lives. Their upward mobility was not without its tribulations or effects on family life.

This is a book all grown up naughty children will enjoy. Chapters with headings like 'What part of NO don't you understand' or 'I don't care who started it' are sure to bring back memories for many, as will sibling rivalry and surviving accidents, poisonings and explosions.

Daughter of a Sea Locked Isle

This is the story of Catherine Qualter born in 1859 in the townland of Gortcloonmore, two miles down a bog road in Claregalway that was so out of the way that it was said to be 'behind God's back'. The Qualter family home was one of eleven limewashed cottages clustered together in the little Gortcloonmore colony on the Lambert Estate which were registered in 1851 in the Griffith Valuation Household Survey which was carried out to determine liability to pay the Poor rate (for the support of the poor and destitute within each Poor Law Union).

Following the Famine years want and poverty continued to be a problem and agricultural families existed as tenants-at-will, subject to the whims of James Staunton Lambert their Ascendency landlord, the will of God and the vagaries of the River Clare. In 1879, the year of 'An Gorta Beag', Catherine left home never to be seen again.

Catherine's story is told against the background of the times and the events in rural Galway that shaped her destiny.

Biography

The Author writes; 'I was born and bread and buttered in Summerhill a hard living area in Dublin. Being north of the Liffey we were 'real Dubliners'. By the mid 40's our Georgian and Regency terraces were advancing into decaying tenements but our wide streets were relatively traffic free and provided us children with an enviable freedom. They also provided hard-pressed Mammy's with hours of peace and quiet because apart from feeding any open beak that darkened the doorway the only time they saw their offspring was when they did a head count at bedtime. Even then it was not uncommon to find a cuckoo in the nest and one of your brood being scrubbed clean by a neighbour!

By my 18th year I knew that I was part of a generation whose future would be on a foreign shore. Ireland, an impoverished country with a dismal economic environment and De Valera's deeply conservative theocratic government would not be able to meet either our aspirations or expectations in the furtherance of a career. Our exodus was rationalized by many families as a temporary expedient until things improved at home but I was realistic enough to know that my exile would be a long one.

Early in the New Year of 1957 I 'took the boat' to start my nurse training in London's East End. Half a century later, after a long career in Public Health Nursing, and despite having Gypsy Feet I have settled into retirement there.

66205675R00083

Made in the USA
Charleston, SC
12 January 2017